The
WHOLE
PET DIET

The WHOLE PET DIET

EIGHT WEEKS TO GREAT HEALTH FOR DOGS AND CATS

Andi Brown

Foreword by Richard Pitcairn, DVM

CELESTIAL ARTS
Berkeley | Toronto

For Voyko
Because of your love,
I found my dream.

Front cover images by David De Lossy/Photodisc Green/Getty Images (dog) and Ingra Publishing/SuperStock (cat)

CELESTIAL ARTS
an imprint of Ten Speed Press
Box 7123
Berkeley, California 94707
www.tenspeed.com

Distributed in Australia by Simon and Schuster Australia, in Canada by Ten Speed Press Canada, in New Zealand by Southern Publishers Group, in South Africa by Real Books, and in the United Kingdom and Europe by Publishers Group UK.

Cover and text design by Catherine Jacobes Design

"Vita-Mineral Mix", "Eye and Nose Drop Formulas", and "Healthy Mouth Formula" from *The New Natural Cat* by Anitra Frazier and Norma Eckroate, copyright © 1981, 1983, 1990 by Anitra Frazier and Norma Eckroate. Used by permission of Dutton, a division of Penguin Group (USA) Inc.

Library of Congress Cataloging-in-Publication Data
Brown, Andi.
    The whole pet diet : eight weeks to great health for dogs and cats / Andi Brown ; Foreword by Richard Pitcairn.
        p. cm.
    Summary: "An eight-week program to optimum health for dogs and cats featuring quick and easy recipes for homecooked meals and treats, a healthy introduction to natural supplements, and a practical guide to grooming and play"–Provided by publisher.
        Includes bibliographical references and index.
        ISBN-13: 978-1-58761-271-8
        ISBN-10: 1-58761-271-2
1. Dogs–Nutrition. 2. Cats–Nutrition. 3. Dogs–Food–Recipes. 4. Cats–Food–Recipes 5. Dogs–Diseases–Diet therapy. 6. Cats–Diseases–Diet therapy. I. Title.

SF427.4.B75 2006
636.7'0893–dc22   2006018284

Printed in the United States of America
First printing, 2006

    2 3 4 5 6 7 8 9 10 — 10 09 08 07

Contents

Foreword

For many years when my veterinary practice was very busy, people would contact my office and get on a waiting list. We would give them recipes for fixing natural and wholesome food, and while they were on this list, they would begin feeding their animals these foods as a preparation to coming in for their first visit. When their name would come up and we called them, we'd often get the response "Well, he's all better now." This just from improving the diet. There's a real lesson in this, isn't there?

Veterinarians are beginning to realize the importance of good nutrition in matters of health, especially as pioneers like Andi Brown bring this to our awareness. Schools of veterinary medicine offer more instruction on nutrition than when I went to school back in the 1960s. Still, it isn't enough considering how critical a good diet is for the health of our pets.

As my training occurred a long time ago, I had to learn this the hard way—by becoming ill myself and slowly getting better through changing my eating habits. It was an interesting learning experience for me to first go to a specialist in internal medicine who put me on a very processed standard American diet—a diet that didn't help me at all. When I took matters into my own hands and began to eat more whole foods, more vegetables, and less meat, and use some nutritional supplements, I found myself on the road to recovery. I also started an exercise program—not much in retrospect, but much more than I had ever done before. Slowly my health improved, enough that I continued to eat this way. Actually, I continued to eat better and better with time, so that now, after twenty-nine years of eating organic foods and a vegetarian diet, I can attest to the real value of this. Perhaps I have been unusually fortunate, but I am very grateful that I haven't needed to be treated by a doctor all these years or take any drugs other than occasional homeopathic treatments.

It was natural to extend this knowledge to the animals I was caring for, and this started me down a different fork in the road. As I began to apply some of my ideas about better feeding to my patients, I again saw positive effects. Sometimes I was shocked by the improvement. I'm embarrassed to admit that, at the time I began to do this, I didn't understand why the fresh-food diet made such a difference. Wasn't the food provided by pet food companies also good? After all, it was all balanced, inspected, based on research, and so on. It was only after years of experience that I began to understand why most commercially produced pet food is inadequate for optimal health.

Andi will explain much of this in this book, which I highly recommend. One of the biggest obstacles for people in making a switch from commercial pet foods to a home-prepared and optimal diet is the feeling of being alone. This book will be your friend in this new adventure—use it and enjoy your pet's improved health.

—Richard Pitcairn, DVM, author of
Dr. Pitcairn's Complete Guide to Natural Health for Dogs and Cats

Acknowledgments

A lifetime of love went into writing this book. I am grateful every day for everyone who has contributed so beautifully to the process. For all of the animals and the people who love them, this work is for you.

Thanks to Becky Johnson for her relentless persuasion in finally getting me to write this book. Your energy, creativity, and research will help make many animals well for a long time to come. To Steve Newman, who finely tuned the process, kept me organized, and continues to make me laugh. To Ginger Betties, my pillar of stability, who picked me up when the chips were down. To my agent, Julie Castiglia, applause for your vision. Cheers to Julie Bennett, my incredible editor at Ten Speed Press, for getting the show on the road, allowing me my freedom, cooking for her slightly overweight cats, and completing our health program so effortlessly. She has "first-paw" knowledge of this diet and its power. To some special friends: "Karen," for keeping me sane and tasting everything we made; Juliet, who produced white light when things looked a little gray; and Chris and Jill, who continue to help guide my spirit. To all of the beautiful "Halo Babes" for their endless enthusiasm and the wisdom they shared with me over the years: Alex Beinart, Cheryl Sprague, Hope Tyson, Miss Scarlett, Sam Haley, Christina Keller, Lynne Megee, Annette Ferrell, Holly Overton, Jennifer Sica, Kenia Norris, Judy Newman, Christie Steele, Rue Smith, and Kay Coppersmith. To the whole production crew: JJ, Alex, Lori, Mike, Gary, and Ben. It couldn't have been done without your help.

To my brother Joel for his constant "clever-whatevers," for the compassion he inspired, and for bringing me the fifty-seven critters that made me who I am. To the greatest sister in the world, who came fully equipped with all the eternal optimism (and John). To Mike and Jen, who always cheered me on. To Dr. Richard Pitcairn and Anitra Frazier, whose works have enlightened and inspired us all. Their books are the bibles for natural pet care. Many thanks to Dr. Gregory Todd, who was there when I needed him most. To my parents, Sylvia and Alvin, who showed me that there was nothing in the world that I couldn't do. To my dear friend Jonathan Kross, who always jumped into the boxing ring whenever it was needed. To Ann Martin, who dared speak the loudest. For the Beach Boys, who continue to sing to me now. And to all of the natural food stores and holistic pet stores that embraced our philosophy over the last twenty years.

Finally, an enormous thank you to all of the wonderful, caring pet owners who contributed their countless miraculous stories and helped validate my work. Your stories were so inspirational. And most of all, to my sweet Spot, Bravo, Jasmine, Sweetie, Kitty, Bijoux, Clem, Love, Peace, Harmony, Mo, Budgie, Budget, Chook, Vwoodgie, Coco, and Vanna, for teaching me firsthand that true love is a wise love.

How It All Started

Ever since I can remember, I've wanted to work with animals. My compassion for all creatures has led me on a very unusual journey. In my lifetime, I have created a way to help thousands of pets and the people who love them, and in this I have found a way to achieve my heart's desire.

In 1986, my cat Spot developed numerous health problems. His symptoms manifested as skin and coat problems, digestive disorders (chronic diarrhea alternating with irritable bowel syndrome), eye and ear infections, fleas, urinary tract and kidney malfunction, an embarrassing paunch, and a hypersensitivity to most unusual situations. I took Spot to five different veterinarians, all of whom prescribed premium foods and prescription drugs, but nothing worked. Over the course of a year, I was told at least three times to just put him to sleep, there was nothing to be done. Then fate took a peculiar turn.

I met Voyko Marx, the warmest, most sensitive and insightful man I've ever known. Knowledgeable about both nutrition and natural health, he immediately began to assess my poor Spot and sweetly inquired, "What's wrong with your cat?"

"It's a genetic disease, and he'll never be cured," I said, a little shaken by his question.

"Well, what are you feeding him?" he asked.

"The best there is. It's what all the vets recommend."

"May I see?"

"Look," I hissed. "It has nothing to do with the food; it's just my cat." I stormed into the kitchen wondering how he could question my devotion, my maternal instincts, my good and honorable intentions, and my knowledge and understanding of pet care, which had been confirmed by all the veterinarians I knew. I grabbed a can of premium diet food and practically threw it at him.

Voyko began scrutinizing the label. (Keep in mind that back in the 1980s, most people weren't reading labels for themselves, let alone their cats.) Within moments of rolling the can back and forth to examine the ingredient panel, he responded, "No wonder your cat's sick, Andi; you're feeding him garbage! I'm going to cure your cat."

Partly seething but mostly curious, I followed him into the kitchen, where he began to prepare a simple stew with chicken and vegetables. That night, with nothing to lose, we sat down to dinner, my very willing cat included, and each ate a big bowl of stew. (That same recipe eventually became Spot's Stew, the signature product of our company, Halo, Purely for Pets.)

During that first week of feeding Spot his new stew, we watched him go through an incredible metamorphosis. Everything about him began to change. His skin cleared up, and the excessive shedding and dandruff disappeared. (I had to quit joking about owning a fur-lined couch.) His digestive system settled down, the fleas disappeared, and the litter box had no offensive odor. He seemed more confident and energetic than I'd ever seen him, and his excess weight melted away effortlessly, yet he was never hungry or crying for food. In a nutshell, my Spot grew into the most gorgeous, healthy cat you could ever imagine! Even Voyko was amazed at how quickly and deeply Spot responded to the new diet.

Real Food Is the Foundation of Life

Nothing on this planet can grow, live, thrive, or flourish without real food. When we eat real, wholesome, healthy, and natural food, like a chicken and vegetable stew, we support every single one of our biological systems at a deep, cellular level and bolster the body's innate abilities to heal itself and resist disease and degeneration. This holds true for people, plants, and animals.

After our experience with Spot, we began intensive research to learn what really goes into commercial pet food. What we found was pretty horrific. Most pet foods on the market contain harmful chemicals and ingredients of inferior quality, such as by-products and fillers (which provide no nutritional value at all). Sustenance perhaps, but hardly healthy or supportive of a pet's well-being. Commercial food is to Spot's Stew as a horse and buggy is to a jetliner; you may get to the other side of town, but you'll never see the world. Commercial foods can keep your pets alive, but they will never provide glowing great health.

Because of Spot's ordeal, we studied centuries of holistic and natural health care, for both humans and animals. We took what we learned and turned it into a vehicle to help others like us, who appreciate the benefits of balance, nature, and love. This book is a compilation of what we learned: when the inside and outside of a body are in balance, good health follows. Real, wholesome, natural food is the foundation to good health; natural supplements provide a push toward balance; and your environment (mental, spiritual, and physical) plays a strong role in overall well-being. By simply modifying our food choices to include only fresh and pure ingredients, we begin the healing process. And when we and those we love are healthy, we are well in our world.

Pets used to get a healthy, balanced diet naturally. You may remember a time when dogs roamed freely and cats prowled the neighborhood at night. Pet food was an unnecessary commodity; scraps from the butcher and the dinner table were the feast du jour. Today, most pets live indoors and the pet industry has exceeded $36 billion annually on products alone. Unfortunately, more money is spent on packaging, processing, and promoting than on quality ingredients to support health. Until recently, we assumed our pets were getting everything they needed in the store-bought foods we gave them. We believed that if the labels claimed these foods were complete and balanced, then they were adequate enough to keep our loved ones healthy. The truth is that most pet foods on the market today do little more than sustain life.

Let's face it, a person can actually live on potato chips and beer. Some people do, but not very well, and not necessarily for very long. It might sustain life to some degree, but it doesn't promote great health. It's easy to make the connection between junk food and human obesity and our common health problems. We need to make that same correlation between the junk in commercial pet foods and pet diseases and obesity.

> **"In speaking with vets that practiced thirty or forty years ago, before the pet industry grew, they state that they did not see the diseases in dogs and cats that we are seeing today. Cancer, liver and kidney disease, allergies, skin problems, all were basically unheard of in pets."**
>
> —ANN MARTIN, author of
> *Foods Pets Die For: The Shocking Truth about Pet Foods*

Manufacturers know all too well that your cats and dogs will prefer to gobble up products loaded with carbohydrates, salts, sugars, and artificial flavor enhancers, so that's how most pet foods are formulated. As a result, pet obesity has exploded to epidemic proportions; according to the National Academy of Sciences, one in four pets is obese. That's a nation of more than nineteen million fat cats and sixteen million flabby dogs. There are over four million websites referencing diabetes in pets and over five million sites on cancer in pets. In the last ten years, we witnessed the birth of the pet insurance industry and its growth into an

$88 million money-making monster. Despite all of this concern and growing awareness of the problem, most people, including many veterinarians, fail to recognize the most fundamental concept: real food is the foundation of life. You are what you eat.

Unfortunately, ailments have become the norm for many pets: liver disease, heart disease, kidney disease, diabetes, skin problems, digestive disorders, tumors, joint and back problems, and a plethora of other health problems. Most pet owners would try anything and spare no expense to keep the ones they love healthy or return them to good health. How many of us have spent hundreds or even thousands of dollars trying different drugs, medications, or surgeries without success? And yet we still keep trying to get different results using the same methods. It's time to try a new approach. If you keep walking into the same wall and all you get is a bump on the head, it's time to try walking around the wall. The answer is simple and inexpensive, and it's right in front of our pets' noses! Most people are unaware that the food they feed their pets may actually be causing their problems.

What's Really in Your Pet's Food?

The shocking truth is there's no watchdog ensuring our companion animals are getting even minimum nourishment. The pet food industry is entirely self-regulated and, sadly, most companies are focused on the bottom line. The government doesn't regulate the quality or sources of pet food ingredients, and pet food companies are allowed to use poor-quality and even dangerous ingredients that barely sustain life and almost never promote great health. Let's take a look at the chief culprits: by-products, fillers, and chemicals.

BY-PRODUCTS

Many pet foods, even the so-called natural ones, may include by-products, which are foodstuffs rejected for human consumption but permitted in pet foods. This includes beaks, feet, feathers, hooves, hair, eyeballs, and bones. Meat rendering plants purchase and process one hundred million pounds of waste material every year, including roadkill, ground-up diseased animal parts, and fecal matter, which can then be incorporated into pet foods and labeled "by-products." "Meat meal" (including chicken meal or fish meal) is a more pleasant-sounding name for such by-products, but it still refers to rendered products from animal tissues (including bone) exclusive of any added blood, hair, hoof, horn, hide, manure, or stomach and rumen contents (except, of course, in such amounts as may occur unavoidably even with good processing practices). Saddest of all, and as truly awful as it sounds, over the years several pet food manufacturers have been caught processing the remains of dog and cat carcasses that have been euthanized, obviously with highly toxic substances, including their pet tags and collars.

FILLERS

Inexpensive fillers, such as corn, wheat, rice, and potatoes, add bulk or volume to a can or a bag. Adding them makes economic sense to pet food makers, but they have enormous detrimental effects on pets. These grains are overused, and their high carbohydrate content and empty calories create a very unbalanced system. Corn is actually the number one ingredient found in common pet foods today, but not only is it difficult to digest, it's the leading cause of obesity in animals. Fortunately, the holistic veterinary community has finally stopped promoting grain-laden foods because they recognize these fillers may be the underlying cause of diabetes and kidney problems, too.

CHEMICALS

So, how does a forty-pound bag of dry food stay fresh in the garage for two months in the summer? Chemical preservatives, such as BHA and BHT, which have been shown to be carcinogenic in laboratory studies, have a significant presence in many pet foods. Although the artificial colors that abound in most treats and semimoist meals make them look appealing to the human eye, they don't impress your pet and may even harm it. Many people and pets are allergic or sensitive to FD&C Red No. 5 and Yellow No. 7. Ethoxyquin, a very inexpensive chemical used in many pet foods as a preservative, is also commonly used as a weed killer and rubber stabilizer. People don't spray their yards with weed killer and let their pets eat the grass, but this substance is found in more pet foods and treats than one could imagine, and many of us are willingly feeding it to our pets every single day.

Hidden Dangers and Misconceptions

Every commercial pet food sold in stores in the United States contains the phrase "complete and balanced" on the ingredient panel. They all actually meet the minimum government standards to sustain life, but keep in mind that the key word here is *minimum*. Many people who buy "premium" pet food snobbishly look down their noses at the thought of buying an "ordinary" brand of food, but most of them wouldn't actually be able to tell the difference between their favored premium brand and the more commercial products. That's because there's usually no difference. Almost every commercial pet food on the market contains a very long list of isolated vitamins and minerals at the end of their ingredient panel. Don't mistake this to mean that these companies are giving you anything extra or care more about your pets. The nutritional analysis must meet certain criteria, but it's usually only achieved by adding vitamins (often derived from synthetic sources) to the product's substandard meat, meat by-products, and fillers. The actual foodstuffs in the product wouldn't meet the minimum standards without them and, as a result, couldn't sustain life, let alone promote health. Let's face it; you don't have to add beta-carotene to a carrot. Like humans, pets need supplements, but we all need to get the bulk of our nutrition from real, wholesome, digestible food.

Pet food manufacturing practices are anything but savory. Plus, anything added to an ingredient before it gets to the pet food plant need not be listed on the label itself, so even the savviest of label readers may be fooled by this heartless industry. Many a brand sold in health food stores may contain chemical preservatives added to the grain before it arrived at the processing plant, so let the buyer beware. Also, salt is added to many foods to mask their inferior quality and get pets to eat it, but this added salt can have enormous repercussions on your pet's kidneys, heart, and liver. In their literature, some products boast that their ingredients are USDA inspected and allude to using high-quality ingredients, but this is just semantics; all ingredients are USDA inspected, but when they're rejected they can still be used in pet foods.

So how do you know whether you're really getting what you're buying? You can't, really, except by monitoring your pet. If your pet has no health problems, looks great, feels great, and makes but one yearly trip to the vet's office, you're probably on the right track—at least for the moment. But keep in mind that as the body gets older, including your pet's, it needs more support to keep it functioning properly. Life is ever-changing and evolving, and our individual needs change, too. The truth is that some animals and humans can live on junk foods and feel just fine, but those with chronic health problems need better nutrition than that available from store-bought commercial foods. It's time to make the connection between what a pet eats and its overall health.

After our success with Spot and our eye-opening investigation of the pet food industry, we became convinced that we should help others restore their pets' health. Our first opportunity came when Fencer, our friend Henry's dog, developed some alarming health problems. We were anxious to put into action what we had learned about cats to see how well the diet translated to dogs' needs. We couldn't have been happier with the results.

Henry and Fencer: Just Open Your Mind

Henry was a local celebrity. As a lecturer, teacher, and scholar, he had a "prove it to me scientifically" mentality. Fencer was a lovable, devoted, twelve-year-old tan and black shepherd mix who had been with Henry since he was a puppy. Fencer had developed a giant tumor at the bridge of his nose that protruded between his eyes and swelled to the size of a baseball. As if that weren't enough, poor

Fencer had also developed arthritis, which was only worsened by the extra ten pounds he carried with him. His low energy level was easy to account for.

Several local veterinarians proclaimed that there was nothing they could do to make Fencer better. The tumor, which festered continuously causing him partial blindness, was too large and Fencer was too old for the operation anyway. The diagnosis was grim: Fencer couldn't be cured, so he should be put to sleep.

Henry asked us if we could help. He was ready to abandon the scientific community's prognosis and take a leap of faith. Fencer had always been fed typical grocery store food loaded with chemicals, fillers, and by-products. Oh, those crunchy little morsels, filled with salty faux cheese and little artificial meat-like-looking things; they have to be the worst! Our distraught friend was ready to do anything it took to help his comrade, so we designed an entirely new, homemade food plan for Fencer, and as soon as it was implemented, the changes came quickly. It's amazing how positively an animal's body can respond when given the right nutritional support.

Initially, we put Fencer on a brief fast of just the broth from our chicken stew. His weight began to drop, which made it easier for him to walk. We gradually added in more solids and several natural supplements, and over the course of the next eight weeks we all marveled at something we never dreamed possible. Fencer's tumor began to shrink measurably each week (from about four and a half inches in diameter to finally about half an inch). It stopped oozing, his vision improved rapidly, and he regained both energy and spunk.

We also made sunshine and exercise a part of Henry and Fencer's new routine. We gave them a second chance that no one thought possible. Henry was grateful to experience the quality of life his best friend regained, and Fencer lived out the next four years with no obvious disease symptoms. Fencer taught us that it's never too late to eat well.

True Pet Stories

In the years since that first experience with Spot, I have been blessed to be a part of an amazing array of success stories like Fencer's and to see the levels of wellness that people have been able to achieve for their pets. Some I knew personally, others only through letters and emails. Throughout this book, it's my privilege to share some of the stories of these wonderful creatures with you. I hope they'll help illustrate the power of the Whole Pet Diet and how the art of great health can produce results that are both concrete and miraculous. All of the natural elements and practices that brought these pets new wellness are a part of the eight-week plan in this book. For example, you'll learn to identify unhealthy pet foods in week one and get rid of them in weeks two and three. You'll learn to make Spot's original stew recipe in week two, and you and your pet will enjoy a play date every day of the eight weeks.

The Labor of Love

Pet owners share an incredible bond with each other, and most claim they'll do whatever it takes for their furry friends. Most of my friends had heard Spot's story, and they were excited about his transformation. Soon we were sharing Fencer's story too, and before long we were sharing our recipe with every pet owner we met. For many of us, cooking for our pet is a labor of love, and it's also one of the best ways to discover the healing power of real food for any being.

Changing your pet's diet isn't just a temporary measure to help it through an illness; it's a lifetime prescription for health. Consider this all-too-common situation: A pet is gravely ill, and the veterinarian prescribes cooking chicken and rice or beef and rice. The anxious and hopeful pet owner races home to makes these prescribed meals and perseveres in this process for a week or two. On their next trip to the vet, the pet is pronounced well and the vet instructs the person to go back to the original food, which again triggers the illness. But this just perpetuates a downward health cycle.

Why not feed the same high-quality, real, wholesome, and healing food as the pet's steady diet, every day of its life? Why should it eat good food only during times of sickness or disease? Why shouldn't our pets be eating healthfully every day to promote optimum health, vitality, and wellness?

Gail and Sam: Make Time for Health

Gail was a close friend with a very full life. Her time was mostly spent being a career woman, keeping her newlywed status interesting, and juggling all kinds of household chores and events surrounding her ten-year-old daughter's school and sports activities. Their other family member was Sam, a four-year-old, purebred black Labrador retriever. Sam fit into the mix and lifestyle of the family with ease. Everyone loved this really great dog who was content just being a part of the group. He was no trouble at all and very low maintenance until . . .

"There's something very wrong with Sam." Over the phone, Gail's voice was frantic. He had been chewing himself raw, biting at his skin, and losing his hair in huge patches. Now beset by copious amounts of diarrhea alternating with vomiting, Sam was becoming dangerously dehydrated.

On top of all this were some equally horrifying vet bills and the challenges of giving Sam medication three times a day for four or five months. They had tried a pill here, a shot there, and even a pricey, prescription-formulated food that was supposed to help him. Steroids had helped his skin problem subside temporarily, but it always came back with a vengeance, and his digestive system worsened. Gail was at the end of her rope. "I can't handle this financially anymore, but even worse is how miserable Sam seems to be," she confessed with obvious tears in her voice. "I think I need to put him to sleep. What else can I do? What would you do?"

I thought a moment, mentally going over all the information on nutrition I had begun to gather in the past few months, then replied, "Chicken stew. You'll have to cook for him."

"Cook for him?" she shrieked. "I don't have time to cook for my family, let alone a dog. I couldn't possibly make that kind of commitment. I have no time. I'll have no life. Give me something else to do—anything but that."

"There's nothing else to do," I said. "The only option is to cook for him. I'll give you an easy recipe. It won't cost much, and you can make it once a week and freeze it, so you won't have to do it every day. Other than that, I have no suggestions."

Within an hour Gail was making Spot's chicken stew for Sam.

One week later, to the day, I received a call from Gail. "You won't believe it, Andi! He's not biting or scratching at himself. His hair is growing back, and there's no more vomiting or diarrhea. He's fabulous again! I can't believe I was actually thinking of putting him to sleep. We love you for helping him so much. I feel so guilty that I even considered the unthinkable."

It's been twenty years, but I still remember that moment as if it were yesterday. Deep gratitude and satisfaction fell over me, and I knew we were onto something big. The excitement was intoxicating, but a week later a very distressed Gail called again with news that knocked the wind out of my sails. Sam had started to bite and chew at himself and the vomiting was back with a vengeance. She just couldn't take it anymore.

Through a haze of disbelief, my mind and my heart raced frantically as I tried to process this new information. "Wait a minute. Didn't you call me about a week ago and say how great Sam was doing? Did I dream or imagine all of that?"

"Oh, yes. Sam was doing phenomenally back then, but once he was better, I put him back on his regular food. . . ." Her voice trailed off.

As the silence stretched between us, I could almost hear her brain making the connection as she came to the realization that real food creates health. With a bit of a whimper in her voice, she asked if she had to cook for Sam forever. "Well, my friend," I replied, "until we get a bigger kitchen, I'm afraid so!"

All too often, people get results from a healthier diet and see a healthier pet, only to revert back to the old food. Gail had to hear herself ask her own question to realize the simple truth: you are what you eat—true for people, and true for pets.

After talking to Gail, I couldn't wait to tell everyone what we were discovering. At that moment, I knew there were no coincidences. We were meant to help the world understand that what people feed their pets is actually either causing their illnesses or making them well. It was one of the greatest moments in my life.

I decided to form my company, Halo, Purely for Pets, as a vehicle to educate people about the importance of diet, nutrition, and natural health for pets. I had to get the word out to everyone that there was new information available and that common health problems that were previously masked with drugs and surgeries could actually be remedied—even cured—with nutrition or preventative measures.

As my quest for knowledge developed, I was fortunate to find a unique book that not only confirmed what Voyko and I were discovering, but also contained vital information we had yet to explore. *The New Natural Cat*, by Anitra Frazier, helped transform our lives dramatically. In the days that followed, we befriended the author, embraced many of her philosophies, and prepared some of her recipes. Soon after, I self-published a booklet entitled *Holistic Pet Care*. To date, that booklet has been sent to more than 600,000 people around the world.

At first, people laughed at us. The notion of natural foods and natural products for pets seemed absurd to many. But great health is unmistakable; you see it in your pet's eyes, its coat, and its energy level. Pretty soon, people started to listen to us talk about how we approached pet care. I even coined the phrase *human-grade* to help differentiate high-quality pet foods from the common, substandard products found in traditional pet foods.

Many years ago, I learned that if you ask a question long and hard, sooner or later the wisdom of the universe shines through and the answers come. It took some dogged determination, and it led me away from mainstream schools of thought, but I found out that it's okay to think outside that "litter box" once in a while. Since that long-ago conversation with Gail, I've learned that my gift is the ability to find natural solutions to common pet problems and my mission is to share them with you.

The Whole Pet Diet Eight-Week Plan

I've carefully developed this eight-week program to introduce the elements of the Whole Pet Plan in a natural order for creating a healthy pet. By following the program, you can transform your pet step-by-step, each week adding a new element while continuing those from the previous weeks. It's important to follow the program in order and also to keep detailed notes about what you experience, so in chapter 2, I'll help you create a Whole Pet Journal, complete with three important forms: a Weekly Checkup list, a Whole Pet Portrait, and a Week at a Glance chart.

Chapter 1 delves into the plan in detail so you can get familiar with the program and what it involves. Chapter 2 describes the principles of my whole pet approach and offers examples of how they work, using elements of the eight-week plan. Chapters 3 through 10 are each devoted to one week in the plan. These will guide you and your pet through the eight weeks, providing tips and insight every step of the way, along with easy-to-make recipes and remedies. Each of these chapters begins with a small, thoughtful project that will help broaden and deepen your understanding of whole pet health.

Throughout the book, I'll share my methods with you and explain the changes and challenges that are likely to occur as you follow these guidelines. More important, I'll help you understand the reasons behind the practices in this book. Throughout, true pet stories will highlight what other healing artists have experienced with their cats and dogs.

After you complete the Whole Pet Diet eight-week program, you'll be able to use this book and your journal as a handy reference tool. It's my hope that many a useful page will be dog-eared so that you can easily find the recipes and remedies you'll need. You can also visit my website (www.thewholepetdiet.com) for further updates, more recipes and remedies, recommended reading and other resources, and frequently asked questions.

Chances are you already know your pet needs my eight-week plan. But if you're still not sure, please take the following quiz.

- Does your pet have a paunch?
- Do you leave food down all day?
- Do you feed dry food?
- Do you give more than one treat at a time?
- Does your pet's food contain by-products?
- Does your pet's food contain sugar, corn syrup, or other derivatives?
- Does your pet's food contain ethoxyquin, BHA, BHT, or other chemicals?
- Do you use chemicals of any kind on your pet, including flea control products?
- Does your pet shed excessively, or only twice a year during shedding seasons?
- Does your pet have a greasy coat, especially around the tail?
- Does your pet have mobility issues?
- Does your pet's energy level need improvement?
- Does your pet attract parasites, like fleas, ticks, and worms?
- Does your pet vomit regularly?
- Does your pet exhibit digestive problems, such as irritable bowel syndrome or constipation?
- Does your pet eat ravenously?

- Does your cat have litter box problems?
- Does your pet eat potted plants or grass?
- Does your pet have offensive body odors or bad breath?
- Does your pet have any chronic eye or ear discharges?
- Is your pet a couch potato?
- Does your pet have skin problems?
- Do you visit the veterinarian more than one time a year?
- Does your pet have diabetes?
- Does your pet have kidney disease or has it experienced kidney failure?
- Does your pet have tumors?
- Has your pet been diagnosed with allergies?
- Has your pet been diagnosed with an immune deficiency disorder or an autoimmune disease?

If you answered yes to two or more of the questions, you and your pet need this book. Whether your pet has seemingly minor problems, like skin irritation, or more serious ones, like diabetes, feline leukemia, or even cancer, you can create a healthier pet. This book's eight-week plan will guide you down a surprisingly short path to health and wellness for your companion animal. Though some of the techniques may seem time-consuming, surely they're easier than endless trips to the vet or watching your steadfast companion suffer.

This book has been designed to help engage your own wisdom in bringing your pet's health and wellness to a level you might never have dreamed possible. Together, we'll create an environment where your beloved pet can be naturally supported in living a longer, happier, and healthier life. We'll work together to unlock the mysteries of your pet's health situation and dispel the myths associated with alternative therapies and natural approaches. High-quality, chemical-free food, exercise, sunlight, clean water, and proper supplementation will help your pet take full advantage of its natural healing abilities. By the time you complete the eight-week plan, everything you do for your pet will be holistic and for the benefit of its entire being.

CHAPTER ONE

The Whole Pet Diet: An Eight-Week Plan to Achieve Optimal Pet Health and Help Prevent Disease

Most of us know the importance of eating healthily and getting plenty of exercise. Putting these concepts into practice and making a lifelong commitment to keep doing so is usually far more difficult. If you're like me, you want to know if something is really working—you want to see the results. I kept this in mind as I developed my eight-week plan, and I promise that you'll start to see the first signs of great health in the first five to ten days. I'll mentor you every step of the way and help you and your pet develop new and healthier habits. As you move through the program, you'll start noticing behavioral changes, and by week eight, your pet will be well on its way to a healthier state of being and a more harmonious way of living. You'll discover why most of the health problems and issues we see in pets today are much more common than you may think, and how easily they can be healed with a more natural diet and a holistic way of living.

The art of great health is about intuition and methods, not just rules. This difference is central to your success, which will hinge on developing your inner pet wisdom. To help shape your work, I'll share my method, the tools I use, and some techniques I've picked up along the way. But as a healing artist, the form you master will be uniquely your own.

The Whole Pet Diet can be applied to every pet at any stage of life. The eight-week plan can help puppies and kittens to grow, develop, and adjust more easily to their new homes, and it can help senior dogs and cats stay active well beyond their "average" life span. But that's only natural, as whole pets are well above average when it comes to great health and vitality and fewer vet visits. Our healthy, homemade stew recipes are designed to allow pets of all ages to feel and look their best. They are perfect foods for perfect pets, and the recipes contain all the important vitamins, minerals, and amino acids in the proportions needed to keep your pet healthy throughout its life. This nutrient-dense diet helps eliminate common problems, such as shedding, allergies, and constipation. It also reduces the risk of debilitating diseases, such as diabetes, tumors, urinary dysfunction, and heart problems. This diet, full of fresh, real food, will regulate your pet's weight and blood sugar levels naturally, ensuring radiant health inside and out.

The Whole Pet Journal

As you progress through the eight-week program, you'll record what you and your pet experience in your Whole Pet Journal. At the end of chapter 2, you'll find the forms you need; simply photocopy them, then put them into a three-ring binder. You'll need three copies of the Whole Pet Portrait, six copies of the Weekly Checkup, and eight copies of the Week at a Glance.

Maintaining a weekly health assessment and behavioral journal will illuminate important connections and help you develop as a healing artist. As you fill in the pages, you'll hone your intuitive healing skills and become better able to step back and evaluate your pet's total health picture. You'll come to know instinctively what is working and what needs adjusting. Beyond the visible results—your pet's radiant health—you'll have a well-documented written and photographic record of the path you followed to achieve that result. As you and your pet continue your life journey together, you can draw on your observations to help your pet live life more fully.

THE WHOLE PET PORTRAIT

You'll take a Whole Pet Portrait three times: at the beginning as a baseline, at the beginning of week five to evaluate your pet's progress, and at the end of the program. Creating a Whole Pet Portrait is about stepping back and viewing your pet in a new light. The portrait will help you focus on your pet's overall well-being while also remaining aware of specific needs. It can help you make needed changes on your journey to creating a healthier pet. The questions in the Whole Pet Portrait are designed to help you evaluate where your pet is, physically and emotionally. They will also help you track and document your progress as you begin to change old, less healthy habits into new holistic ones. In addition to this written portrait, take photos or videos of your pet along the way. Most people are so astounded by the results they achieve that they're grateful to have documents that reveal how far they've come. By the time you finish taking your third portrait, it will become obvious to you that you and your pet are well on your way to a new, healthier way of life. Taking additional portraits throughout the rest of your pet's life will help keep you in tune with how to help your companion age gracefully.

WEEKLY CHECKUP

The Weekly Checkup is a mini version of the portrait. You'll fill it out at the start of weeks two, three, four, six, seven, and eight. This checklist helps you look closely at your pet's eyes, ears, skin, coat, mobility, energy, disposition, and digestion. You'll also do a weekly weigh-in, complete with belly measurements.

WEEK AT A GLANCE

This handy chart provides a place for you to record your pet's meals, snacks, supplements, and other nutrients throughout the week. You'll also record how much exercise your pet gets each day, along with details on any medications.

WEEKLY ASSESSMENT

At the end of each week, you'll answer a series of questions at the end of the chapter specifically about that week's focus and project to ensure that you understand and successfully progress through the program. Add loose-leaf ruled paper to your journal for doing the weekly assessment, as well as for noting any other changes you see in your pet and writing down any thoughts or ideas that occur to you as you work through the program.

Your Weekly Whole Pet Diet Routine

I highly recommend that you establish a weekly routine for the program. For most people, starting each week on a Sunday makes sense because they have the day off, but feel free to choose another day if it better suits your schedule. Here are the essential steps for each week of the eight-week program:

- Read the chapter for the week.

- Complete either the detailed Whole Pet Portrait (when starting week one and week five) or the shorter Weekly Checkup (when starting weeks two, three, four, six, seven, and eight).

- Do the recommended weekly project. Try to start the project on the first day of the week. Read the description and do your best.

- As the week progresses, log your daily play dates in the Week at a Glance. Ideally, you should do this each day so you don't miss, forget, or skip a date.

- Log *all* of your pet's daily food intake in the Week at a Glance: this includes meals, snacks, table scraps, vitamins, supplements, any prescription medications, bites out of plants, ill-gotten gains from hunting, socks, slippers, or anything else you know your pet has consumed over the course of the day. Ideally, you should do this every day so you don't forget a single morsel.

- At the end of each week, complete the Weekly Assessment. Describe what happened with the project, how your pet improved, and any changes in your pet's energy levels, behavior, or eating habits.

Here's a preview of what you can expect to be doing each week in the program.

WEEK ONE: THE ART OF EFAs

You'll start week one by creating your first Whole Pet Portrait. Then you'll begin nourishing your pet's skin and coat from within by adding essential fatty acids (EFAs) to each meal. Your project for the week is to study the ingredients in whatever you're currently feeding your pet—and the marketing pitches that try to convince you these products are healthy.

WEEK TWO: THE ART OF THE STEW

In week two, you'll start to truly transform your pet's diet with our homemade stew and other healthy preparations served on a regular feeding schedule. Your project is to toss out all the commercial pet foods with low-quality pet-grade ingredients.

WEEK THREE: THE ART OF THE TREAT

Your pet will love week three. You'll offer nourishing treats as energy-boosting snacks and as bribes to ease the transition. I've provided a wide range of treat ideas and recipes for you to choose from, from the easy to the elaborate. Your project is to hunt down and toss out all the commercial treats you may have stashed around the house.

WEEK FOUR: THE ART OF THE SUN

In week four, you'll add the healing power of green foods: cereal grasses and other plants rich in chlorophyll, beta-carotene, and protein. Your project is to take inventory of all chemical gardening products or poisonous plants that could harm your pet and either remove them or take safety precautions.

WEEK FIVE: THE ART OF WELL B-ING

In week five, your pet will begin to benefit from the calming, healing support of B vitamins. You're halfway through the program. At the beginning of the week, you'll take a second Whole Pet Portrait and compare it with the first. Your project is to make a vitamin-mineral powder that's easy to add to meals for both your pet and you.

WEEK SIX: THE ART OF IMMUNITY AND HEALING TOUCH

In week six, you'll boost your pet's immune system with vitamin C and other antioxidants. Your project is to introduce the healing power of touch as you massage your pet.

WEEK SEVEN: THE ART OF HEALTHY TEETH AND BONES

Week seven focuses on stronger teeth and bones, with a bonus of fresher breath! You'll learn about natural dental care for your pet and remedies and preventive measures for arthritis and other joint problems. Your project is to get rid of any commercial "teeth-cleaning" foods, chews, or toys that don't safely deliver what they promise.

WEEK EIGHT: THE ART OF THE SPA

You'll end the eight-week program with a holistic spa day, pampering your pet with a healing bath, grooming, eye and ear treatments, and more. Your project is to remove any commercial pet shampoos and flea treatments with harmful ingredients. The program concludes with a final Whole Pet Portrait so you can see all the healthy changes in your pet.

Daily Play Dates: The Art of Exercise

Holistically speaking, play is as important as diet. It will help you bond with your pet and stimulate a great mental and physical relationship. I'm asking you to set aside a block of "Wheeeee!" time with your pet every day for the sheer health of it! As you begin the eight-week plan, you need to schedule a ten-minute playtime each day of the week.

That's right, enter it in your calendar or PDA now: at least ten full minutes every day to do nothing but wrestle and roll with your pooch or bat around a favorite toy with your cat. If you can't afford ten minutes a day, you can't afford to keep your pet healthy—get a fish. Lap petting as you watch TV, or the "duty walk" with your dog during which you're talking with a friend or (especially!) on your cell phone, does *not* count as playtime. On a real play date, your pet gets your full attention and engagement, one-on-one. So grab a ball, a sock, some catnip, a fancy feather, or whatever your pet loves to play with and go for ten full minutes. You can do more, but you must not do less.

Need some ideas? Take your dog to a new doggie park or for a swim in the ocean. That great sea air is full of ions that are beneficial to both of you. Don't live near the sea? Try visiting a lake or a river or going for a run in the woods. Got cats? Set up a string of grocery bag tunnels and design a kitty gym. However you can manage to do it, go out and enjoy a good laugh with your favorite friend. Try to bring out your pet's sense of humor. Believe me, it's there. Don't be afraid to let the silly side of you out; your pet will love it.

Start and end playtimes consistently, establishing a routine. Pets function very well within a schedule; it helps with feeding times, potty breaks, and, as mentioned here, play dates. Committing to a daily play date and making it fun for both of you is nurturing and nourishing. It gives you a chance to listen to your inner pet as well. Play, like laughter, is one of the healthiest gifts we can give our bodies. For pets, play is literally the heart of good health, and part of your job as caregiver is to commit to your pet's total well-being. Don't let anything or anybody encroach on this sacred space in your busy day. It's soul time for both of you.

Cat Safety Caution: Don't give your cat any plaything that you wouldn't give a child younger than age three. Make sure that all toys are safe and don't have harmful parts that could be swallowed and lead to choking, such as buttons, bells, and yarn or string. Toys should be played with under your close supervision and taken away when playtime is over.

Dog Safety Caution: Be careful that you don't give your dog anything that could cause choking. Make sure that all of its toys are sturdy. If toys are torn or worn and losing filling, throw them away. Many dogs are rushed to the vet because they've swallowed fiberfill from their soft toys. Dogs should never be allowed or encouraged to rip open plush toys, especially those with squeakers, which are especially dangerous if swallowed.

We humans have learned about our own health through many years of observing what animals do instinctively. All those stress management techniques we read about in health magazines for people—meditation, exercise, stretching, playing, resting, fasting—are what most animals do naturally if we let them. Think about it; every time your favorite feline gets up from a catnap, it stretches. It usually begins with the front paws extended, and then the back hunches, the neck drops, the stomach pulls in, and the tailbone tucks under. If this sounds like a yoga posture, it is, and it's called Bidalasana, or the cat pose. Cats usually finish off the stretch with a game. They might hop atop a dresser and bat around some loose change or play tetherball with the mini blind strings before plopping down on your newspaper or curling up on a favorite pillow in the middle of the bed. Who said cats don't meditate?

Dogs, on the other hand, will chase Frisbees, socks, sticks, balls, and even their own tails if you just say the word *go*. And when they become overheated, they'll lap up plenty of water or cool off in the shade of a tree. Most pets will instinctively get their heart rate into their "target zone" if you let them. They'll also naturally take time to stretch and cool down after a workout.

Always try to work aerobic exercise into your play dates; it's a great way to ensure your dog or cat gets moving and breathes healthfully for at least a little while each day. Ten minutes a day is a good starting place, but as you progress through the eight weeks, I'll ask you to increase the frequency to twice a day and increase the duration to fifteen minutes or more each time. On weekends or days off, see if you can commit to even longer; the more play, the more exercise, and the healthier your pet will be. Vigorous exercise helps to move toxins out of the body and supports the lymphatic system.

Want to know what a dramatic difference regular play dates can make to your pet's health? Read the true story of Debbie and Cleo.

Debbie and Cleo: Move It!

Cleo was a basset hound with a big problem (and I mean big*). At eight years old, Cleo tipped the scales at a whopping 105 pounds, though ideally she should have weighed about 60. This sweet, gentle dog with ears that leisurely dragged on the floor mystified the experts with her continuous, ravenous appetite. Although obesity is a problem for any dog, with short legs and a long back, this particular breed is already predisposed to all kinds of joint and musculoskeletal problems, which are only compounded by the extra weight.*

Debbie tried all kinds of reducing diets and even withheld food from her precious baby, but nothing made any difference. Cleo was always hungry.

Cleo's weight began to diminish her ability to walk, and soon it became impossible for her to even move around the house on her own. She ate meals lying down, and except for her long ears, she was starting to look a little like a walrus. Debbie and her husband did their best with Cleo, maneuvering her into a makeshift sling to take her outside to relieve herself. Cleo was mortified, and the strain was becoming too great for Debbie as well, both physically and emotionally.

Debbie is the kind of pet owner I most often encounter, an "I'd do anything for my pet" person at her wit's end and hanging onto a shred of hope for some kind of miracle turnaround. Luckily, she had heard about my work from a friend.

"Cleo is so unhappy," she cried. "I can't bear to see her suffer anymore. Her joints hurt, she howls when she moves, and she's getting

worse. I have an appointment with my vet to put her down tomorrow. Is there anything you can do for her? We love her so much."

It's always a shock to my system when a pet owner reaches the point of no return. I was determined to help Cleo get a new leash on life. The first thing I always ask is what kind of food the animal is eating.

"I've used all kinds of dry foods on her," sobbed Debbie. She had tried everything the vet recommended and wanted me to know she had done all she could.

"Well, first, I never recommend dry food," I said. "Dry food is always grain based, which is what causes so many pets to put on excess weight. Many obese pets, and humans, are actually starving. The grains are empty calories filled with unnecessary carbohydrates, and most pets are ravenously hungry because of this. It's kind of like being on a potato chip diet; you could probably eat an entire bag, but you would never feel full. For the body to be satiated, it needs high-quality nutrients like meat and vegetables. These are absorbed and utilized by the body, they feed the organs, and they enable the digestive system to eliminate waste gracefully. You need to start cooking natural food for Cleo and incorporating enzymes and antioxidants. This will help bring oxygen to the cells, which should increase her energy."

Debbie was willing to try one more time with this new concept under her belt. I suggested that she feed Cleo the chicken and vegetable stew and also incorporate a high-potency multivitamin, enzymes to aid digestion, and additional vitamin C to bring oxygen to Cleo's cells. Debbie was eager to get started and promised a detailed report twice a month.

Within the first two weeks, Cleo lost seven pounds. After a month, Cleo's weight was down by nearly fifteen pounds. She could eat her food standing up, and for the first time in a year, she was actually able to walk, albeit slowly, from one room to the next. Toward the end of week five, Cleo walked outside totally unassisted. By the end *of the second month, her energy level had increased even more dramatically. The progress was contagious, and Debbie scheduled two twenty-minute walks around the neighborhood with Cleo every day. As Cleo proceeded on her new diet regimen, she continued to show signs of improvement. Her joints limbered up, and by the end of the tenth week Cleo bounded out the door with Debbie and her husband for a glorious trot through the neighborhood. Three months later, Cleo had shed an impressive thirty pounds and the whole family began running together in the park.*

The last time I spoke with Debbie, she thanked me profusely for the wisdom we brought to her whole family. You see, Cleo wasn't the only one who needed to lose weight. Both Debbie and her husband shed some unwanted pounds in the process. "Don't thank me," I said, "thank Cleo."

Animals can teach us so much. To this day, Cleo's whole family is still jogging down the road to wellness.

Keeping an Eye on What Comes Out

Achieving great health is an art—one that is all about balance and harmony. As you begin your eight-week journey, you'll learn immediately that it's important to assess every aspect of your pet's life. What your pet eliminates from its body is as important as what it takes in, so it's essential to keep a watchful eye on these functions. Stool frequency and condition and urinary patterns are a true testament to what's going on in your pet's system. Believe it or not, I have worked with many people who initially tell me things like "my dog has cancer, but other than that he's really healthy" or "my cat has kidney failure, but she's really in great shape" when the pet's elimination was signaling otherwise many times each day. To illustrate the importance of the clues that a pet's output provides, I'll end this chapter with the story of Scarlett and Booda.

Scarlett: Awakening the Booda Within

Scarlett was all about health, nutrition, and yoga when she was adopted by her new boyfriend Renaldo's sweet, petite, and oh-so-fluffy gray Persian cat, Booda. The slow but purposefully moving Booda was so pretty, it was hard for Scarlett to convince Renaldo that keeping him on dry food was anything but healthy. He used to argue that he couldn't really justify food supplements, much less the pricey, canned human-grade pet food. His argument was "Come on, he's a cat! And just look at him; he's amazing already."

After a few months of dating this lovely cat and having to put up with the somewhat stubborn boyfriend as well, Scarlett noticed that there seemed to be problems in the litter box. Scarlett found blood in Booda's stool on a regular basis, and the poor, regal seven-pound cat seemed to strain way too long when moving his bowels. To make matters worse, the odor from the bathroom was so vile it could clear out the house. Booda would drink water nonstop. Scarlett's Zen training had taught her that great health begins with a natural and balanced diet, and she figured the same had to hold true for this cat. It was time to take charge of the household.

She clearly remembers the day she decided to "put her paw down" and insisted on tossing the kibble. She replaced it with my chicken stew, and Booda took to the new food with fervor. Over the next couple of weeks she watched Booda's transformation.

Scarlett loved how this glorious creature draped himself lovingly over her head every night as they slept. In the mornings the two arose early, and to Scarlett's delight, Booda would race to the kitchen to get a jump start on breakfast. "I loved seeing him run through the house like a kitten again, skidding and sliding across the long tile floor." The chicken stew did wonders for him in every way: physically, emotionally, and spiritually. Booda's thirst appeared to be quenched by the bountiful broth of the stew, and he no longer drank copious amounts of water. No one noticed when he used the litter box, as the smell had disappeared, and they never saw blood in his stool. His wondrous gray coat grew even thicker and more luxurious than it already was. It was even easier to care for; it matted much less and shined more than ever. Oh yes, Booda was even more Booda.

Nothing worthwhile is easy. There were times when Scarlett needed to travel, and the notion of leaving dry food for two days seemed okay. It only happened twice, she told me, because even after he ate dry food for only a day or two, Booda's constipation would return and so would the blood and that awful odor. Scarlett realized it was far healthier for Booda to forgo food for a day than to be subjected to the grain-based dry product that seemed to disagree with his body in every way.

The inspirational cat was always close by and seemed to join in as Scarlett performed her daily yoga rituals of stretching and meditation. Sometimes it felt as though the two began breathing as one. How lovely to have such a positive effect on another being's life.

Renaldo and Scarlett parted ways after a while, but Booda went on to live with Scarlett in her new house. Scarlett continued to work with Booda throughout his life, and as the lovely cat aged, Scarlett was tuned in enough to listen to his body and choose additional supplements to support his health and help him feel good. Her sweet Booda was treated royally for many more years, and together, they continued to prove the timeless wisdom that you are what you eat.

In the next chapter, get ready to open your mind and let the principles of real health flow in. It's much simpler than you may think. Together we'll help your pet achieve the optimum life you may have only dreamed about.

CHAPTER TWO

The Art of Great Health

The eight-week plan outlined in this book is a creative process that binds you and your pet more closely together and unites body, mind, and spirit for each of you. It's a lifestyle change that returns you and your pet to a more natural, wholesome way of eating, moving, breathing, and living. When we promote peace and harmony in our lives, we positively affect every cell in the body and create a healing physiology. This healing art strengthens the immune system, calms the nervous system, and can even change our attitudes, emotional state, and perception of pain. In other words, the art of creating great health for your pet is transformational, and I believe, transcendent.

The Whole Pet Diet originated with the illnesses of my cat Spot and several close friends' pets, but it was quickly elevated to a fine art when a very special puppy, an Australian shepherd named Bravo, entered my life. My healing experience with Bravo illustrates the whole life benefits of the whole pet approach, and his story is interwoven with the following descriptions of my most important principles. I already understood the power of real food and how it could benefit animals whose health was compromised by low-quality, commercial, pet-grade foods. I wondered what my already magnificent Bravo would grow into if we took a whole pet approach with him. For Voyko and me, exploring just how fabulous a totally holistic dog could be was the next and most natural step of our path. We were already into nutrition, herbs, fasting, and meditation for ourselves, and the more we worked with animals, the more we saw that similar lifestyle changes could be enormously beneficial for them, too. Before long, our kitchen and, soon after, our house were entirely devoted to providing natural care and healthful food for cats and dogs. When we changed how we viewed our pets' world, our own world changed completely.

One day, I noticed Bravo was scratching incessantly. I checked his skin, and he definitely had some sort of irritation. I also noted he was eating less and wasn't as energetic as usual. I suspected chemicals had infiltrated his system and later, while watering the garden, I discovered a hole he'd dug underneath the fence. No doubt he'd been rolling in the neighbor's yard, and probably eating their grass. I couldn't blame him. The thick, beautiful, dark green St. Augustine lawn was certainly inviting. But it wasn't altogether natural: I remembered that my neighbor had mentioned a yellow spot full of chinch bugs he had to treat with insecticide. That evening I checked Bravo's stool, and sure enough, it was a bit green and much softer than usual. I could tell that his immune system was weaker, too, because he was starting to attract fleas and was drinking more water than normal. (What I learned from Bravo's brush with insecticides is the basis for the project you'll do in week four.)

To look beyond Bravo's symptoms, we did what we always do: extensive research. We learned what he needed to support the ballistic movement of his body, energize his curious mind, and lift his joyful spirit. Our success came from simple practices: providing great food and a clean environment, and understanding how to create harmony in the body so it can heal itself. Our approach embraces homeopathy (the philosophy that like heals like), and remains open to all alternative therapies, such as acupuncture, aromatherapy, Bach Flower Remedies, energy healing, feng shui, and massage, some of which are incorporated into this eight-week plan. You might say we balanced the conceptual healing arts of Mother Nature with physical clues to develop our basic principles.

The Basic Principles of Great Health

Our plan for healthy pets is based on four principles: balance, conscious feeding, guidance, and love.

BALANCE

Holistic health is the philosophy that all things are connected. The inside of the body, the outside of the body, and the environment must be in balance to achieve harmony. Just like us, pets need love, quality nutrition, sleep, clean air, fresh water, exercise, sunshine, and positive emotional and spiritual surroundings. It's important to understand that when pets display physical disease symptoms, such as skin disorders, ear or eye problems, or even fleas, they are simply out of balance in one or more of these areas. By stepping back and looking at the whole pet, you can see what is out of balance and what you can do to bring it back into alignment naturally.

Taking care of a physical or bodily need, like ensuring more sunlight for that cat who hides in the closet or the dog who only gets walked at night, often aids an animal's emotional or mental acuity, thus lifting its overall health. There is significant potential that one change can bring balance to many needs, and the following list illustrates some of the connections in the balancing process.

- *Physical needs:* real, wholesome, delicious, and satisfying food; exercise and play; sunlight; pure water; stool health; hugs and pets; grooming; a safe place to rest.

- *Emotional needs:* love, compassion, and forgiveness; hugs and pets; grooming; a purpose in life or a "job"; companionship; sunlight; real, wholesome food; a snug retreat.

- *Mental needs:* stimulation of all the senses; a sense of responsibility; wholesome food; positive thoughts; exercise and play; sunlight; fresh air; naps throughout the day.

- *Spiritual needs:* calm, quiet times; fresh air; closeness to nature; love; hugs; naps and a good night's sleep; cleanliness; opportunities for service, such as guarding, providing warmth, or being a greeter or a hostess.

I believe harmony is found in the blending of opposites, much like the Chinese philosophy of yin and yang. In the middle of hot and cold is a comfortable warm temperature, just right for bathing your pets. They need sunlight and play, and also darkness and rest. You might blend the sweet taste of pineapple with the sourness of yogurt to heighten your pet's digestion, or alternate vitamin C with a vitamin B complex to balance its pH levels. We need to understand that both opposites are equal in importance and necessary for harmony.

To bring Bravo back into balance, we first filled the hole he'd dug and fixed the fence. To heal him from the outside, I rinsed his coat thoroughly with water then used a castile shampoo with a couple of drops of an herbal flea potion added in for good measure. For a week I misted him with this herbal flea spritz every time he came in from the outdoors. Voyko prepared a plate full of live enzymes, protein, and supernutritious green foods to soothe Bravo's stomach and heal the inside of his body.

CONSCIOUS FEEDING

Food is the foundation of life. This is my most basic principle. I know it's radical to think of food as medicine and to imagine that those expensive, colorfully bagged kibbles and canned pet food pâtés are destroying the health of your companion animal, but the art of great pet health depends upon nutritional enlightenment. In reality, food as medicine isn't a new or a radical concept. Hippocrates, the father of modern medicine, expressed this view 2,500 years ago. He understood that true health requires a balance of body, mind, and environment, and that disease is caused by a disharmony in one or more of these areas.

The power of food to heal disease is dependent on the quality of food, and that's why every recipe and remedy in the Whole Pet Diet includes the freshest, most environmentally safe ingredients you can grow or buy. Be conscious of everything you put in your pet's mouth or on your pet's body. I wouldn't give anything to my pets I wouldn't eat or use myself.

Our conscious feeding of Bravo incorporated plain, organic yogurt to benefit his intestinal tract, along with a raw organic egg and some freshly chopped parsley to help the nutrients assimilate into his system quickly. We also added a little chopped garlic to his dinner: Mama's healthy homemade chicken stew.

Conscious feeding moves beyond ingredients to include clean bowls and cleared eating areas. Get your pet accustomed to eating only at mealtimes. This means no more free-feeding. Your pet will have a better appetite and more vitality, and will also build better bones and blood and a stronger immune system during the rest of the day. Ending free-feeding will also help an overweight pet slim down more naturally and prevent your pet from getting bored with its food. Both cats and dogs should be fed twice a day, and food should be removed between meals (with homemade, high-quality food, dogs will typically finish in a few minutes; allow thirty minutes for each cat's meal). You can make an exception for sick or elderly animals and kittens and puppies, which may eat smaller, more frequent meals, perhaps three or four times a day.

Sometimes a caregiver is locked into the one-meal-a-day mind-set. Oftentimes, vets lead us to believe feeding less, in amount, duration, and frequency, helps our pets lose weight. This isn't true. Feeding too little or too seldom will slow your pet's metabolism and can lead to weight gain. Achieving an ideal weight is less about quantity than about the quality of the ingredients and the body's ability to assimilate as well as eliminate the food. I like the two-times-a-day regimen to separate digestive times. Plus, it's easier on their bodies and our schedules.

When your pet is done eating (or when your cat's thirty minutes is up), remove the bowl. This is important, because a pet's olfactory sense activates the digestive process. Every time an animal smells or eats food, vital blood and oxygen supplies rush to the stomach to aid in digestion. This process diminishes the amount of oxygen that reaches all the other organs and actually causes the body to age prematurely. Leaving food down is actually against the laws of nature. Pets' bodies need to rest, have mini fasts, and not be in digestive mode all the time.

Many pet owners are initially unnerved by the notion of not leaving food down all day. Some even develop the fear that their pet might somehow starve if it didn't have access to food for a few hours. However, not eating is nature's way of promoting healing.

In nature, most animals function on a feast and famine diet, and often the strongest cats or dogs are those who have eaten as natural or as close to nature as possible, which for some means eating wild prey. In a recent conversation with the editor of *Cat Fancy* magazine, even I was surprised to learn that the oldest cat they knew about lived thirty-eight years. (That's one healthy pussycat!) She was a true barn cat, living solely by hunting the mice that regularly invaded the horse's grain bin. Wild animals don't have a tidy little dish of mouse or bird waiting to be eaten, and most wild animals don't even eat every day. Nature has a way of keeping them fit on less fuel: first the animal becomes hungry, then it finds its prey. As it begins to stalk the prey, its body revs up into the hunting frenzy, preparing itself for digestion. Licking its chops stimulates saliva production, and the smell and sight of food increases its heart rate and thus its metabolism. If the predator isn't a seasoned hunter, sometimes it misses its prey and has to repeat the process while experiencing the famine cycle.

Most holistic vets I know recommend a full day's fast each week for a normal, healthy dog or cat. If you're paying attention, you'll notice that many pets fast naturally, sometimes for an entire day at a time. This allows Mother Nature to do her job and cleanse the body of impurities. By ensuring that the body doesn't spend most of its time in the digestive process, fasting helps to keep the body healthier and stronger. Nature intended animals to work hard for their meals and not have food available all day. On the domestic flip side, house pets who casually stroll to the food bowl throughout the day to eat overly processed, pet-grade foods may show tendencies toward maldevelopment, constipation, weight gain because of a slower metabolism, and poor skin condition, as well as a slew of other problems. These problems are all too common for the majority of sedentary American pets that spend much of the day sleeping.

GUIDANCE

Making nutritional changes in one area will often spark a healthier change in another. Our eight-week plan is a template, a starting point, for whole pet healing. Unfortunately, this is not a one-size-fits-all program. As you start feeding your pet whole, healthy foods, allow your senses to guide you through the healing processes. This book is designed to give you confidence in your ability to observe your pet's changing symptoms and make gradual modifications to its diet as needed. Your pet may initially prefer foods with salt, sugars, or other "flavor enhancers," but the elimination of those unhealthy additives will promote obvious, exciting changes in its physical and emotional well-being. In time, your pet will prefer the natural, nutrient-dense choices you provide.

My eight-week plan includes all the tools and tips you need to get in touch with your own inner pet so you can fine-tune the recipes and remedies to your pet's individual needs, wants, and tastes. You want to make this a pleasurable experience. After all, you're not starting with a blank canvas or a still life; you're retouching a living, breathing masterpiece. You need to pay attention to each animal's own special needs to help bring its body back into balance.

I knew Bravo needed the healing power of garlic to help get rid of fleas and boost his immune system, but I also knew from previous taste tests that he didn't care much for the smell or taste of it. So I learned to add just a little fresh garlic to each bowlful of the stew that he loved. It's often more effective to sneak a helpful-but-disliked ingredient into your pet's favorite main meal or treat than it is to directly dose them with it.

As he ate more garlic, Bravo's skin cleared up, his scratching stopped, there were no more signs of fleas, and his stool looked fine. But his energy hadn't returned to normal, and I was worried about his compromised immune system because rainy winter weather was on the way. I also wanted to return his coat back to its original luster. We gave him a raw marrow bone to chew so he could create more of his own digestive juices and clean his teeth naturally (as you'll learn about in week seven). I also added some extra vitamin C and vitamin B complex to every meal. (You'll start giving your pet these water-soluble vitamins in weeks five and six.) We also served Bravo a shake made with liver and greens (see page 141 for the recipe) twice a week for the next month.

In no time at all, my beautiful Bravo was back in balance.

LOVE

Rest easy, I know you love your pet. If you didn't, you wouldn't be reading this book. I believe every great work of art is inspired by love, and surely this is more relevant to the healing arts than any other art form. This powerful emotion is the true healer that unites body, mind, heart, and soul. Be very kind to yourself and your pet, and you'll soon discover a joyful new way of life, a natural way of seeing, thinking, and being.

Practicing kindness and paying attention often raises our awareness, and becoming aware is not always easy. As we begin to fully understand the whole pet, we begin to see how far modern life has taken our pets, and us, from our natural environs, and how advertising and the multibillion-dollar pet products industry has oppressed pets as a group. We must be persistent and continue to read, study, and question everything involving the health and well-being of our animals. We must challenge old ideas, like "kibble is good," and current trends, where animals are dressed in bathing suits and treated as a fashion accessory. We must find new, more compassionate ways of living in harmony with our animal companions. As we raise our own consciousness, we raise awareness, and this not only benefits the whole pet—it benefits the whole planet.

The external herbal remedy I'd concocted for Bravo did its flea-banishing work, but the bath was also a wonderful opportunity to lavish loving attention and touch on my sweet boy. The welcome-home aromatherapy spritzing ritual I devised for him ensured that Bravo got a loving greeting upon entering the house. (I'll provide full details on these and other nurturing grooming rituals in week eight.)

Make a Whole Pet Commitment

I wrote this book to help you make wise choices. Only you can determine the degree of wellness your pet achieves, and whether you want your pet to just survive or to thrive. Please start by accepting yourself and your pet's health wherever you are at this very moment. Never blame yourself for what happened yesterday, or for what you didn't know last month. Be joyful that tomorrow is a new and healthier day, and that each week of this program will move your pet closer to glowing, radiant health. In this spirit, I invite you to commit yourself to these principles:

- I will change my behavior and the choices I make to give my pet great health.

- I will make conscious choices to do what's best for me, my pet, and the environment.

- I will choose high-quality, human-grade products and never stoop to lower-quality, pet-grade standards again.

- I will go the full mile in my commitments and not take shortcuts.

- I will find a veterinarian who supports my natural choices and truly cares for my pet and me.

- I will continue to learn more about natural health for my pet and the holistic approaches available.

It's Never Too Late to Create a Masterpiece

If your pet is aging or overweight, or has chronic health problems, you might be thinking that it won't do any good to start applying the principles of great health now, that it's already too late. But it's not! The doorway to wisdom is always open. As the story of Whisker proves, it's never too late to eat well.

Whisker: The Diabetes-Food Connection

Sanjay thought his lovely cat Whisker was just getting old. At fourteen, Whisker was diagnosed with diabetes and prescribed insulin for the rest of his life. Over the course of the following year, Whisker's doses of insulin steadily increased until he was up to three units two times a day. Poor Whisker went from a robust thirteen pounds down to ten pounds very rapidly. His once-shiny coat became dry, matted, and lifeless, requiring increasingly frequent trips to the groomer.

This turned out to be a blessing in disguise, as a thoughtful and compassionate groomer helped change their lives forever. She suggested that Sanjay add my blend of vegetable oils, which is high in essential fatty acids (EFAs), to Whisker's food to help with his coat. (See chapter 3 for more on this oil blend.) She assured Sanjay that these oils contained nothing that could hurt Whisker or complicate his issues. Sanjay's vet wasn't particularly enthusiastic about trying the nontraditional remedy and cautioned him that the change in diet might require a change in insulin dosage. Whisker's entire family discussed the possibilities together, and fortunately they weren't deterred by the vet's warning. Sanjay told me his family was already open to new human treatments that might not be accepted yet by mainstream medicine, so it was natural to believe that an alternative treatment might help Whisker, too.

This was around the time when I had the great pleasure of speaking with Sanjay personally. I suggested that, in addition to supplementing with the oil blend, they change Whisker's food from a grain-laden product to Spot's chicken stew, which contains only meats and vegetables. I explained that grains turn to sugar in a pet's body and can wreak havoc on the pancreas and create a need for synthetic insulin shots. The entire family was eager to support Whisker's new program, which they started right away.

After three months of eating only the chicken stew, along with the oil supplement and a selection of green foods (you'll learn all about these in week four), Whisker was proclaimed diabetes-free by his vet. He regained the weight he'd lost and grew out a glossy new coat, and all of his blood sugar curves moved back into normal range. It had never occurred to Whisker's family (or even the vet) that diabetes could be a curable disease. I am still in touch with Whisker and his family and enjoy the wisdom they've shared with me over the years. Because they were sympathetic, not apathetic, their cat is no longer labeled "diabetic"!

Remember, dogs and cats are primarily carnivores, and neither species would prefer to consume large amounts of grains in the wild. Yet most commercial pet foods contain an overabundance of grains, such as corn, wheat, rice, or potatoes. Since we know that high-carbohydrate diets tend to raise pets' blood sugar levels, it's easy to see that synthetic insulin probably wouldn't be needed if grains were eliminated from a pet's diet. When an animal eats a more natural, high-protein diet, its pancreas is able to function normally and create the proper balance of insulin on its own. The addition of green foods is beneficial as well, because they help detoxify the liver, thus enabling the entire body to perform more efficiently.

So, are you ready to change your pet's life and save money? Many people throw good money after bad when it comes to their pet's condition, buying expensive special foods that don't work. Unfortunately, pet-grade products rarely address the real problems, much less reduce the need for vet visits and prescription medicines. When a method works, there should be visible results. I can unequivocally say that I have never known a dog or cat who is eating my homemade chicken stew to be overweight. There is nothing about the body that cannot be changed or improved when given the right nutritional support. To begin the process of true healing, look beyond your pet's symptoms to identify the root problem. Seek new sources of information, believe in yourself, and trust in your own intuitive wisdom. Just look at how Brandi's life changed when Judy stepped in to help her heal.

Brandi, What a Fine Dog You Could Be

Brandi was the dog of Judy's dreams. Judy loved telling me about her adorable four-year-old West Highland white terrier and referred to her as an old soul, a wise one, and a teacher. At eight months old, Brandi took a plane trip to New York to visit family, for which the vet suggested tranquilizers. Shortly after the trip, Judy noticed blood in Brandi's stool. Brandi began vomiting, developed a urinary tract infection, and grew lethargic. The vet ran some blood tests and called Judy within a few hours, urgently telling her that Brandi had Addison's disease. Brandi's sodium-potassium balance was out of whack and she likely had only two hours to live if they didn't stabilize her. By the time Brandi arrived at the hospital, the vet had prepared a protocol of prednisone tablets and Florinef to combat the Addison's. It took nearly two days to stabilize little Brandi and control her violent shaking.

Judy is my favorite kind of pet owner because she wants to know about everything her dog is taking. A vegetarian herself, she understands the importance of healthy eating, so she had always fed Brandi natural dog food. When Judy saw that Brandi's condition wasn't improving much, she went to the library to read everything she could about Addison's disease and the medications her beloved dog was taking. She discovered that the dosage of Florinef prescribed by the vet was much too high according to the drug company's literature.

"Brandi's not getting better, her blood chemistry isn't stable, and she's still vomiting up her food," Judy told the vet. "I've read that Percorten injections are the drug of choice here, and I'd like you to try that."

Because the vet had limited experience with Addison's, he agreed to use Percorten instead of Florinef. Within two days, Brandi's condition improved. They agreed to continue the injections once every four weeks.

About a year later, Brandi developed a crippling case of luxating patellas, a painful and crippling kneecap irregularity. Judy was advised that surgery to correct the problem was out of the question because of a conflict between the meds Brandi was on for the Addison's and the anesthesia necessary for surgery. Additionally, Brandi had gradually become overweight due to ongoing use of prednisone. Judy was advised to trim Brandi's weight to lessen the strain on her knees.

Judy tried doggy acupuncture, and while it seemed to help a bit, this little dog's fate took another turn. Brandi developed struvite stones in her bladder. There was blood in her urine, her white blood cell count was high, and Brandi's need to urinate constantly was unnerving both of them. Judy guessed that the drugs Brandi was taking, and especially the combination of all of them together, couldn't be good on a long-term basis, and she couldn't wait to take Brandi off the antibiotics.

Judy never stopped searching for answers, and her search finally brought her to me. Against her vet's advice, she stopped feeding Brandi the prescription diet he'd recommended and started using my chicken stew. She supplemented Brandi's diet with vitamin C, essential fatty acids, and highly nutritious green foods daily. Although Judy was understandably anxious about what might happen to Brandi, she was certain that her dog wasn't happy in her current state of health, which seemed to slide ever downward in spite of the constant medications. After only one month, I heard from Judy that Brandi no longer had symptoms, had lost a total of three pounds, and had a perfect score on her blood work. And at last, Judy had been able to decrease Brandi's prednisone dose dramatically.

Judy was ecstatic. "Brandi's eyes are bright, she's sleeping soundly, and she's not begging for food. She's playing with her toys and comes running to my husband when he arrives home from work. Although I gave up dreaming about the dog she could have been a long time ago, she has finally become the dog she was meant to be: healthy, happy, and perfect."

Judy's vet asked her what she had done to get Brandi into such great condition, and when Judy told him about the program, he didn't suggest modifying her medications, which I find disturbing. As Brandi's body changes and strengthens, Judy continues to have Brandi's blood work monitored, hoping she'll need fewer drugs on a regular basis.

Judy's story is a good example of why it pays to never stop searching for answers when it comes to your pet's health.

The Whole Pet Diet Is for Life

The Whole Pet Diet is not about deprivation and indulgence. It's about a holistic way of caring for and feeding your pet so it will live a longer, healthier, and happier life. You are already an extraordinary healer, and I want you to trust you'll know right where to look and what needs your attention. As you move forward, try to stay as close to Mother Nature as possible; this means understanding her rhythms and recognizing their effects on all living creatures. Remember that her rhythms, like her colors, vary in intensity and are intricately linked to life cycles and emotional states. Think of the ebb and flow of the ocean, the flames and embers of a fire, and the very breath of life. As with everything in nature, our pets' bodies go in and out of balance. As you progress through this book and fill in your Whole Pet Journal, your awareness of these cycles and balances will increase. You'll develop a special way with your animals and fine-tune your eye for creating a healthier life for your pet. And the sooner you begin, the quicker the healing process takes place, so let's get started!

The following pages contain blank versions of the forms you'll use to create your Whole Pet Journal. Make three copies of the Whole Pet Portrait, six copies of the Weekly Checkup, and eight copies of the Week at a Glance. Place the copies in a binder and add loose-leaf lined paper, and you're ready to begin the eight-week program.

WHOLE PET PORTRAIT

PET'S NAME: _____

AGE: _____

DATE: _____

1. **WEIGHT:** If you can't get your pet to sit still on a scale, first weigh yourself, then pick up your pet and stand on the scale together. Subtract your weight from the total and you'll have your pet's weight: _____ pounds, _____ ounces. Compare this to the weight in any previous portraits.

2. **My pet is currently** (check one):

    ❑ OVERWEIGHT   ❑ UNDERWEIGHT   ❑ PERFECT WEIGHT

3. **BELLY MEASUREMENT** (measure around your pet's stomach): _____ inches.

4. **APPETITE:** Describe how your pet eats its food (check one):

    ❑ NO GUSTO   ❑ HEALTHY APPETITE   ❑ APPEARS RAVENOUS

5. **MAIN MEALS:** What are you feeding your pet (check all that apply)?

    ❑ KIBBLE   ❑ SEMIMOIST   ❑ COMMERCIAL CANNED

    ❑ HOMEMADE   ❑ RAW   ❑ NATURAL

    ❑ PREMIUM   ❑ OTHER:

    _____

    _____

    _____

6. **PORTIONS:** How much food is your pet consuming in a day (check one)?

    ❑ MINIMAL AMOUNT   ❑ RECOMMENDED PORTION

    ❑ MORE THAN RECOMMENDED

7. How many times a day do you feed your pet (check one)?

☐ ONCE   ☐ TWICE   ☐ THREE TIMES

☐ MORE   ☐ FREE-FEED

8. What kinds of supplements or vitamins do you give your pet and how often?

_____

_____

9. What kind of snacks does your pet consume daily and how often (check all that apply)?

☐ COMMERCIAL TREATS   ☐ HOMEMADE TREATS   ☐ HUMAN SNACKS

☐ ONCE   ☐ TWICE   ☐ THREE TIMES

☐ MORE OFTEN

10. WATER CONSUMPTION: Ideally, your pet should be consuming foods with a high water content. How much water does your pet drink daily and how thirsty does it seem (check one)?

☐ ALWAYS THIRSTY   ☐ TAKES A FEW GULPS   ☐ DRINKS AFTER EXERCISE

☐ SELDOM DRINKS

11. EYES: Healthy pets have clear and bright eyes, including the white portion. Describe your pet's eyes (check all that apply):

☐ CLEAR   ☐ IRRITATED   ☐ WHITE

☐ YELLOW   ☐ RED   ☐ SWOLLEN

☐ DISCHARGE   ☐ TEARING

12. Are you using any specific eye treatment? If so, describe it:

_____

_____

13. EARS: The ears of a healthy pet should be dry, clean, and generally light pink in color, and have no distinct odor. Describe your pet's ears (check all that apply):

☐ DRY   ☐ MOIST   ☐ DIRTY

☐ IRRITATED   ☐ SWOLLEN   ☐ BLOODY

☐ LIGHT PINK   ☐ RED   ☐ MITES

☐ NO ODOR   ☐ BAD ODOR

14. Are you using any specific ear treatment? If so, describe it:

_____

_____

15. TEETH: A healthy pet's teeth are white and tartar-free. Describe your pet's teeth (check all that apply and provide details):

☐ WHITE   ☐ YELLOW   ☐ TARTAR

☐ LOOSE   ☐ BROKEN   ☐ MISSING

_____

_____

16. GUMS: Healthy gums are pink and free of debris; swollen gums or bleeding gums are signs of imbalance. Describe your pet's gums (check all that apply and provide details):

☐ PINK   ☐ WHITE   ☐ RED

☐ BLACK   ☐ BLOODY   ☐ SWOLLEN

☐ LODGED WITH DEBRIS   ☐ ABSCESSED

_____

_____

17. CRAVINGS: Pets with nutritional deficiencies may crave strange substances. Is your pet eating anything unusual (check all that apply)?

☐ ROCKS   ☐ PLANTS   ☐ GRASS

☐ STOOL   ☐ LITTER   ☐ PAPER

☐ PLASTIC   ☐ DIRT   ☐ OTHER

_____

_____

18. BAD BREATH: A healthy pet's breath reflects the quality and freshness of the foods it's eating; it should be pleasant. Describe your pet's breath (check one):

☐ FRESH AND CLEAN   ☐ STALE   ☐ SOMETIMES UNPLEASANT

☐ CHRONICALLY AWFUL

19. **NOSE:** A dog's or cat's nose should be cool and usually one solid color. A dry or cracked nose and odd or irregular pigment can indicate a compromised immune system. Describe your pet's nose (check all that apply):

❑ COOL ❑ HOT ❑ RUNNY

❑ DRY ❑ CRACKED ❑ BLACK

❑ ODDLY SPOTTED ❑ OTHER _____

20. **SKIN:** A healthy pet's skin is white or pinkish, clean, clear, and smooth. Describe your pet's skin (check all that apply and provide details):

❑ WHITE ❑ PINK ❑ RED

❑ BLOODY ❑ IRRITATED ❑ SCABBY

❑ ITCHY ❑ HOT SPOTS ❑ PIMPLES

_____

_____

21. **PARASITES:** Healthy pets don't attract parasites. What kind of parasites, if any, are a problem for your pet (check all that apply and provide details)?

❑ FLEAS ❑ TICKS ❑ WORMS

❑ MITES ❑ MANGE

_____

_____

22. **COAT:** A dog's or cat's coat should feel healthy to the touch. Describe your pet's coat currently (check all that apply and provide details):

❑ SHINY ❑ DULL ❑ SMOOTH

❑ OILY ❑ DRY ❑ MATTED

❑ MISSING ❑ SUPPLE ❑ OTHER

_____

_____

23. **SHEDDING:** Healthy coats shed very little. Describe your pet's shedding (check all that apply and provide details):

❑ SHEDS DURING SEASONAL CHANGES ONLY ❑ SHEDS A LITTLE

❑ SHEDS A GREAT DEAL OF HAIR ❑ SHEDS CHRONICALLY

❑ OTHER:

_____

24. **DANDRUFF: This is a sign that the body is trying to rid itself of toxins through the skin. Does your pet have dandruff (check one and provide details)?**

❑ MILD DANDRUFF ❑ DANDRUFF IN CONCENTRATED AREAS

❑ HEAVY DANDRUFF ALL OVER

❑ WHERE:

_____

_____

25. **BODY ODOR: Healthy pets smell clean and fresh and have no strong odors. Describe how your pet currently smells (check one):**

❑ CLEAN ❑ SOME ODOR ❑ STRONG ODOR

❑ OFFENSIVE ODOR

26. **SORE SPOTS: As you run your hands over your pet's body and apply a little pressure, do you detect any sore or tender areas in its joints or muscles (check all that apply and provide details)?**

❑ HEAD ❑ NECK ❑ CHEST

❑ ABDOMEN ❑ BACK ❑ LEGS (WHICH)

❑ FEET (WHICH) ❑ RUMP ❑ TAIL

_____

_____

27. **LUMPS: As you run your hands over your pet's body, do you detect any lumps or growths that may be bothersome to your pet or that concern you? If so, where are they, and how big are they (check all that apply and provide details)?**

❑ HEAD ❑ NECK ❑ CHEST

❑ ABDOMEN ❑ BACK ❑ LEGS (WHICH)

❑ FEET (WHICH) ❑ RUMP ❑ TAIL

_____

_____

28. **SKIN IRRITATIONS: Is your pet continuously scratching, licking, biting, or chewing any part of its body, and can you see any irritations? If so, where does it occur (check all that apply and provide details)?**

❑ HEAD ❑ EARS ❑ NECK

❑ CHEST ❑ ABDOMEN ❑ BACK

☐ LEGS (WHICH)   ☐ FEET (WHICH)   ☐ RUMP

☐ TAIL

_____

_____

29. **MOBILITY. Healthy pets are flexible and move about gracefully and easily. Does your pet have areas of stiffness that need your attention (check all that apply and describe where in as much detail as possible)?**

☐ LEGS   ☐ JOINTS (WHICH)   ☐ HIPS

☐ SPINE   ☐ FEET   ☐ SHOULDERS

_____

_____

30. **What movement is being impeded (check all that apply)?**

☐ RUNNING   ☐ JUMPING   ☐ WALKING

☐ SITTING   ☐ CLIMBING STAIRS   ☐ GETTING IN THE CAR

☐ STANDING UP

31. **FATIGUE: Healthy animals have plenty of energy and play often. Describe your pet's energy level (check all that apply and provide any details):**

☐ PLAYFUL AND FRISKY   ☐ ENJOYS SOME PLAY   ☐ TIRES EARLY

☐ NOT PLAYFUL   ☐ LETHARGIC   ☐ OTHER

_____

_____

32. **SLEEPING PATTERNS: Get to know your pet's sleep patterns. Is your pet a sound sleeper, or is it restless and uncomfortable (check all that apply)?**

☐ SOUND SLEEPER   ☐ RESTLESS   ☐ SLEEPS A LOT

☐ NORMAL SLEEPER

33. **MOODS AND DISPOSITION: Healthy pets should be generally happy, playful, and easy to be around. Aggressive, fearful, lethargic, destructive, or even overly shy pets may be experiencing a nutritional imbalance. Describe your pet's disposition and provide details if necessary (check all that apply):**

☐ HAPPY   ☐ ENERGETIC   ☐ PLAYFUL

☐ TRUSTING   ☐ SWEET   ☐ EAGER TO PLEASE

☐ OUTGOING   ☐ OBEDIENT   ☐ SAD

☐ FEARFUL   ☐ DESTRUCTIVE   ☐ BITES

☐ SCRATCHES   ☐ AGGRESSIVE   ☐ HIDES

☐ BARKS OR MEOWS EXCESSIVELY

_____

_____

34. **STOOL: This is one of the best indicators of a pet's overall well-being. Your pet's stool should be solid, brown, and tubular in shape, and have no bad odor, blood, or mucus. Describe your pet's stool (check all that apply and provide any details):**

☐ YELLOW   ☐ BROWN   ☐ BLACK

☐ OTHER COLOR   ☐ LIQUID   ☐ RUNNY

☐ SOFT   ☐ FIRM/TUBULAR   ☐ DRY/HARD

☐ CONTAINS MUCUS   ☐ BLOODY   ☐ NO STRONG ODOR

☐ VERY BAD ODOR   ☐ SOLID   ☐ SEGMENTED

☐ OTHER

_____

_____

35. **BOWEL MOVEMENTS: These should be easy and there should be no signs of constipation, irritable bowels, or irritation around the rectum or anal glands. Pets with difficult bowel movements are consuming foods that are difficult to digest and process. Describe your pet's bowel movements (check all that apply and provide any details):**

☐ EASY   ☐ DIFFICULT   ☐ STRAINS

☐ SEEMS PAINFUL   ☐ TAKES A LONG TIME TO ELIMINATE

_____

_____

36. **URINATION: Pets should be able to eliminate gracefully. Straining to release or an extreme change in frequency may indicate a serious health problem and your veterinarian should be consulted as soon as possible. Urine should be clear with a slightly acidic aroma, and it should be free of any blood. Describe your pet's urine and ability to eliminate (check all that apply and provide any details):**

☐ CLEAR   ☐ CLOUDY   ☐ BLOODY

☐ STRONG ODOR   ☐ NO ODOR   ☐ STRAINED/PAINFUL

☐ EVEN STREAM   ☐ ONCE DAILY   ☐ TWICE DAILY

☐ MORE OFTEN THAN USUAL   ☐ LESS OFTEN THAN USUAL

_____

_____

37. **IMPORTANT JOURNAL NOTES:** If you have any areas of concern about your pet's health that aren't covered above, list them here. Any ongoing issues with your pet should be reviewed as you create each portrait to monitor whether your pet is getting healthier:

_____

_____

38. **GOALS:** Describe in detail what you feel would make your pet perfectly healthy. What do you want to change, and what would you like to see happen? I believe there is nothing about the body that can't be changed or improved when it's given the right nutritional support. Use the space below to paint a verbal image of how you'd like to see your pet manifest glowing good health.

_____

_____

39. **PHOTOGRAPH:** Affix a photograph of your pet here so you can easily compare it with earlier and later portraits.

WEEKLY CHECKUP

DATE: _____

WEIGHT: _____ BELLY MEASUREMENT: _____

The checklist below is designed to tune you in to your pet's health from a general perspective. Take a few moments to observe where your pet is this week, then check the symptoms or answers that match best. You can get more specific on the lines provided below. Feel free to elaborate on anything that's unusual or that prompts your concern.

EYES: Clear and clean, Irritated, Discharge. Improving or Same as last week?

_____

_____

_____

EARS: Clean and fresh, Odorous, Dirty. Improving or Same?

_____

_____

_____

SKIN: Clear, Irritated. Improving or Same?

_____

_____

_____

SHEDDING: None, Light, Medium, Heavy. Improving or Same?

_____

_____

_____

DANDRUFF: None, Mild, Heavy. Improving or Same?

_____

_____

_____

ITCHING/SCRATCHING: None, Sometimes, Constant. Improving or Same?

_____

_____

_____

MOBILITY: Strong, Average, Weak. Improving or Same?

_____

_____

_____

ENERGY: High, Medium, Low. Improving or Same?

_____

_____

_____

DISPOSITION: Happier, Sadder. Improving or Same?

_____

_____

_____

STOOL: Firm, Soft, Hard, Mild odor, Strong odor, Contains mucus, Bloody.
Improving or Same?

_____

_____

_____

WEEK AT A GLANCE

Meals: For all that apply, describe what your pet ate.							
	Sun.	Mon.	Tues.	Wed.	Thu.	Fri.	Sat.
Breakfast							
Snack or mini meal							
Dinner							
Snack							
Supplements or Vitamins							
EFAs (week one)							
Greens (week four)							
B Vitamins (week five)							
Vitamin C (week six)							

Supplements or Vitamins							
	Sun.	Mon.	Tues.	Wed.	Thu.	Fri.	Sat.
Glucosamine and chondroitin (week seven)							

Medications

Details

Exercise and Daily Play							
	Sun.	Mon.	Tues.	Wed.	Thu.	Fri.	Sat.
How long?							
Activity							

Best Play of the Week

_____

_____

_____

_____

_____

_____

_____

CHAPTER THREE

Week One:
The Art of EFAs

In your journal:

- Take your first Whole Pet Portrait.

- Schedule your daily play dates.

- Throughout the week, fill in the Week at a Glance.

- At week's end, complete the Weekly Assessment at the end
  of this chapter.

In our very first week, we provide a single, simple response to the most common pet problems and most frequently asked questions: Why does my dog scratch all the time? What can I do about all this shedding? What is my cat allergic to? It's not surprising that the most common and chronic issues relate to the skin and coat, as these provide some of the most visible information about a pet's health. The good news is, pets exhibiting this wide range of symptoms may simply be lacking essential fatty acids in their diet.

Thousands of years ago, priests and physicians in ancient Egypt used precious oils in spiritual and religious rituals, as did masters and seers in India. The Bible abounds with references to the powers of oils in both healing and anointing. Today, we most often associate the healing use of oils with massage or aromatherapy, but this is far too limiting. I believe we are just beginning to rediscover how important oils are to both people and pets. It's no wonder that all manner of oils are showing up in everything from herbal flea remedies to natural cleaning products. But as we begin week one, I'd like you to focus on some specific edible oils as essential nutritional supplements to your pet's diet.

Essential fatty acids (EFAs) may well be the most important supplement you can add to your pet's food. You can quickly create a healthier pet by adding a nutritionally rich oil supplement to any pet food. Eventually, this eight-week program will help you switch to a wholesome diet, but this baby step leads the way. Not only will EFAs give your pet's coat a healthy shine, they'll also help stop shedding, itching, dandruff, hot spots, and allergy symptoms, and they can eliminate the need for cortisone shots and steroids. The most important EFAs for your pet's optimal skin and coat health occur in pure edible vegetable oils, such as wheat germ, sunflower, safflower, and soy oils. They not only are palatable, but also contain abundant amounts of critically important linoleic and linolenic acids, which I have found to work faster and deeper than anything else to turn pets' health around. Some fish oils can be equally beneficial, and the fish flavor may help your pet adjust to this addition to its diet.

Statistics indicate that roughly three-quarters of the dogs in this country make regular trips to the veterinarian's office for costly treatment of allergy symptoms, for which prednisone pills are dispensed like candy. These expensive and powerful drugs may temporarily suppress uncomfortable symptoms, but they can also cause immune system failure, wreak havoc on internal organs, and leave pets unable to stave off infection and disease. In fact, these drugs fail to address the real problem: a lack of EFAs in the diet. Most pets show marked improvement within the first week of consuming a mixture of high-quality oils rich in EFAs. When the ingredients are chosen wisely, my recommended oil blend will produce ongoing, continuous results.

This week, you'll be adding my Recipe for a Beautiful Coat, which is loaded with EFAs, to every single one of your pet's meals. EFAs are indispensable nutrients your pet's body can't produce, so they must receive an adequate supply from the foods they consume. These extremely important nutrients assist every cell in the body to become healthier, and they're critical for normal growth and function of all muscles, nerves, and organs.

What to Expect

Dramatic changes in your pet's skin and coat! You'll notice less shedding and scratching and watch a dull coat begin to glow. Allergy symptoms will become a thing of the past, and you can be sure your pet is on its way to a life free of expensive and dangerous cortisone shots and steroids. Continue to add my oil supplement to every meal throughout the eight weeks (and for life), and you'll be certain to see ongoing improvement in your pet's skin, fur, nails, paw pads, immune system, assimilation, and elimination.

Before you start giving your pet the oils, you need to create your first Whole Pet Portrait to provide a baseline. I can't tell you how often people tell me that they wish they'd taken a picture of their pet before they started the program. Think of the Whole Pet Portrait as painting a picture of the health of your pet as you start on this journey together. Creating this portrait now, again after week four, and again after week eight will allow you to observe how your pet improves over the course of the program. Now's the time to take out the journal you created at the end of chapter 2 and fill in all the details of your first Whole Pet Portrait.

Project: Perception versus Reality

Your project for week one is to observe, research, study, and reflect. Go to your pantry and pull out all the different foods and treats you give your pet. I'm not asking you to throw anything away (at this point); I just want you to increase your awareness. At this early stage, it doesn't matter if you're feeding dry, semimoist, or wet food, and it doesn't matter whether you bought the food at a health food store or a Wal-Mart. Read the labels and make a list of all ingredients you don't recognize. Make a commitment to research all ingredients on your list and find out what you can about them before the week's end.

Next, closely observe how those products are sold to you and all the promises they make about your pet's health. Chances are you've been fooled by Madison Avenue's clever marketing ploys. Pet ads make good television; they show prime chunks of choice beef, fresh fish fillets, a cornucopia of vegetables, and supposedly healthful whole grains before they cut to an animal running energetically through a wooded glen hurrying home for dinner. Every manufacturer claims to have scientific proof as to why their food is the best, but do they? You must educate yourself about the reality, and the sickening truth that the government only requires that pet foods be 12 percent digestible!

We sometimes forget that the proof actually *is* in the pudding. Logically, if what your pet is currently eating really works, you probably wouldn't be reading this book. Perhaps you use a "reducing" dog or cat food, but your pet is still overweight. Maybe you have a product that "enhances the coat" or is good for hairballs, but your cat still sheds horribly and throws up after eating.

Pay attention to the empty claims in television commercials and don't skip over pet food ads in magazines. This is a psychic shift designed to awaken your intuitive self. It's like noticing the fun people have in fast-food commercials and considering it in light of the alarming evening news reports describing how genetically modified organisms (GMOs) and certain fats in those very same types of foods can be harmful.

Most importantly, write down what you're really feeding your pet. Don't forget to include the treats as well as the food.

Essential Fatty Acids

Essential fatty acids (EFAs) are indispensable nutrients our bodies cannot produce and are solely derived from the foods we consume. These "good fats," as they've come to be called, play critical roles in both energy production and cellular membrane health throughout the body. EFAs are vital for the normal growth and functioning of all muscles, nerves, and organs. And since the skin is the largest organ in the body, EFAs are especially important for pets with skin problems, and supplementing them can be highly beneficial for an animal's skin, fur, nails, and hair.

Symptoms of EFA deficiency or imbalance include itchy, scaly skin, excessively dry hair or hair that falls out in patches, cracked paws, split claws, fatigue, weakness, frequent infections, allergies, hyperactivity, depression, learning problems, slow wound healing, aching joints, poor digestion, high blood pressure, and obesity. The most prevalent and easily observed symptoms of EFA deficiency are the first few mentioned, related to the skin and coat. Even if you do nothing else but add essential fatty acids to your pet's diet, you'll see miraculous changes in its skin and coat, often in the first five days.

Make the connection between the most common pet ailments and their cause, and treat that cause, not the symptoms. Instead of treating shedding or skin problems with a different shampoo—an external topical approach that addresses the symptoms—just add EFAs to your pet's food. Because everything is connected, the outside of the body is a direct reflection of the inside, and you'll start to see real, long-lasting changes. When your pet's skin and coat improve, imagine what's happening to the health of its heart and digestive tract. You're assisting overall body function and promoting a stronger immune system.

The Essential Combination

There are two types of EFAs, omega-3 and omega-6 fatty acids, and both are necessary in a healthy pet diet. A little later in the chapter, I'll give you my Recipe for a Beautiful Coat. This is a great source of EFAs, as well as vitamins A, D, and E. When you feed this elixir to your pet, you'll directly benefit its skin, heart, eyes, and immune system. Much better than those synthetic vitamins sprayed onto so many brands of kibble to meet minimum standards, these delicious and fresh nutritional oils can easily be poured over any dry food to make a more nutritious meal and produce a much healthier coat right away.

The benefits of EFAs are bountiful, as are the scientific descriptions of the various EFAs (which I happily avoid). What you need to know for your pet's overall optimal health is this: pets need a 1:2 ratio of omega-3s to omega-6s. This is a little more technical than I like, speaking more to science than to art, but a 1:2 ratio is easy to calculate. If your supplement has 1 percent omega-3 and 2 percent omega-6, you are right on target. Common ratios in pet and people diets are more along the lines of 1 to 30, which greatly overbalances the system with omega-6s and promotes obesity.

One last technical point to consider for omega-3 fatty acids is that there are three important omega-3 fatty acids: alpha-linolenic acid (ALA), eicosapentaenoic acid (EPA), and docosahexaenoic acid (DHA). Don't sweat the long names; just remember that dogs and cats cannot use ALA, so only EPA and DHA are useful as omega-3 supplements in their diets. If you'd like to forget about those complicated names altogether, just remember this: The best source of usable EPA and DHA for pets is cold-water fish, including cod, mackerel, salmon, sardines, and trout. I use cod liver oil in my EFA blend because it's easy to obtain, it's relatively nonperishable if stored properly, and it supplies larger quantities of the needed EPA and DHA.

The Dry Food Factor

What's a key culprit in all those skin problems our pets seem to suffer from? Think about it: "dry food" is not a misnomer. It has less than 10 percent moisture and mostly consists of coarsely ground grain in the form of pellets. It may start with decent enough ingredients, but it's cooked at very high temperatures and then dried into hard nuggets. Even natural brands bake at such high temperatures that the beneficial fats and oils (critical to the coat, skin, and overall health) break down during the process and are rendered useless or even harmful. If it's hard, dry, and crunchy, how is it going to provide beneficial oils to the body? Let's face it, there's no such thing as a "kibble tree" in the wild! It doesn't take a rocket scientist to understand that dry foods can cause many hair and coat issues. That was certainly the case for a golden retriever named Lucky.

Lucky: Anything But

Sad little Lucky—at three years of age, this smart, loving dog was diagnosed with the severest of allergies. Amy tried everything she knew of to help her poor dog, but expensive cortisone shots and prednisone pills did nothing to permanently heal him and Amy worried that using them long-term was bad for Lucky's health. Lucky scratched himself raw at the base of his tail, and scabs and sores popped up all over his body. He never seemed to stop licking his feet, and his coat felt brittle and dry all the time. No matter how much she brushed him, there was never a shine, and although Amy tried medicated shampoos, oatmeal baths, sprays, and every topical coat product she could find on the market, nothing seemed to help.

Lucky came from a long line of champions and Amy had hoped to someday be able to show him, but he never looked healthy enough to come close to the ring. Amy resigned herself to the fact that Lucky would never compete with the other dogs in his class, and because he seemed so miserable most of the time, she often thought of just "putting him down."

Lucky for Lucky, Amy heard me on the radio while she was driving to work. I was talking about the epidemic of skin and coat problems. A frantic Amy dialed the station from her cell phone and asked if I could help her sweet dog. "What kind of food are you using?" I asked right away. She replied that it wasn't the food, it was simply her dog. I tried again. "Are you feeding dry food?" I asked. "Well, yes. It's the good food from my vet. I use only the best," she responded.

In all of the years I've spent talking with countless pet owners, I've come to the realization that everyone believes they are giving their pet the very best care possible. I can relate to each and every one of them, because twenty years ago I felt just the same.

I believed the root of Lucky's problem was the lack of oils in his diet. All that dry food can leave a pet's body depleted. Amy contacted me a few days later and told me that closer scrutiny of the ingredients in Lucky's food revealed that it was loaded with chemical preservatives. We talked more about changing the diet, the importance of pure foods, and, in Lucky's case, supplementing with lots of oils to kick-start the healing process, and Amy agreed to give it a try.

Amy witnessed the miraculous effects of essential fatty acids firsthand. Within the first week of supplementing Lucky's food with healthful oils (including wheat germ, sunflower, safflower, and soy, as well as a double dose of garlic), he had completely stopped scratching. It took close to a month, but eventually his sores healed, and a long, thick, glowing golden coat began to grow. At the end of three months, Lucky was a new dog. Within a year, this magnificent creature even took his rightful place on the show circuit. Everyone asked where she had gotten her new dog, and the trophies lined up in her home. Lucky got lucky because his mother got answers. Amy addressed the cause and not just the symptoms.

Cats and EFAs: A Special Need

Unlike dogs and humans, which are both omnivores, cats are obligate carnivores and require meat to survive. They have a particular need for arachidonic acid, a fatty acid prevalent in animal fat. Arachidonic acid plays a vital role in cats' fat utilization, energy production, and skin and coat health. It's an essential fatty acid for cats because they can't manufacture it in their bodies; they must consume it from food—that is, from meat. So what does this mean for cat owners? It means cats need to consume high-quality EFAs and high-quality meat.

There's another common cat affliction that you can relieve with EFAs: hairballs. Since cats are so fastidious in their grooming rituals, they spend a great deal of time licking and cleaning themselves all over. Cats that are fed a healthy natural diet, complete with a daily dose of EFAs, will rarely have hairballs. Long-haired cats that groom themselves may experience them occasionally during the shedding season, but the shedding season only occurs twice a year. Nature intended most furry animals to have a summer coat and a winter coat to accommodate temperature changes. If your kitty is vomiting hairballs all year round, it's most likely exhibiting dry skin and excessive shedding, too. You should be able to run your hand over your cat's back and come away with little to no hair either on your hand or floating in the air. If you're coming away with a handful of hair, your cat is an ideal candidate for essential fatty acid supplementation.

Let's look at the cause of this problem. Hairballs are clumps of fur that may get stuck in the digestive system. They can clog up the body and could cause blockages. Hairballs are created when a cat cleans itself and ingests loose hair. Addressing the cause is the surest way to eliminate the problem. When you add important fats and oils back into kitty's food, you'll eliminate the excessive shedding, and thus the loose hair your cat is ingesting. Don't be tempted to just treat the symptom with petroleum-based hairball remedies or hairball-formula food. These products contain mineral oil, which deplete the body of the fat-soluble vitamins A, D, and E. Most of them are tested on cats for only a few weeks, so we don't know the long-term effects. Get to the cause of the problem and understand the tremendous role that dry food plays in creating this problem.

Beyond supplementing kitty's diet with EFAs, stay on a healthy grooming schedule. Brush your cat regularly at changes of season (or anytime your cat is shedding) and give your long-haired cats daily attention. Stay on the side of prevention, and you'll never go wrong. Diet and grooming should do the trick. If not, get your kitty to the vet quickly, especially if it's constipated or refuses food for more than a few days.

Let's meet a cat whose voluminous shedding problem was solved with my favorite EFA blend. Then you can mix up the recipe for *your* shedding kitty.

Cashmere: The Cat with a Coat for All Seasons

Jeff told me that he was "king of the lint brush." Every morning, before racing out the door for work in a frenzy, he ran that sticky rolling pin over his suit to collect the cat hair. His friends joked that it would be easier for him to move than to vacuum the copious amounts of fur from every corner of his home. Jeff adored entertaining and took pride in his home, but he was embarrassed because of the hair. He even resorted to covering the furniture with sheets so that people wouldn't mind sitting down. "You couldn't wear black without coming away with a tush full of hair," he said. Cashmere, his cat, was quite sweet and innocent, of course, but this beautiful smoke-colored, long-haired Angora was becoming the bane of his social life.

Sometimes the process of distancing yourself from your surroundings enables you to better focus attention on what needs attention, and this was certainly the case for Jeff. After a three-week vacation, he had an eye-opening experience that made him aware of how bad the hair problem was. As he entered his home, his heart seemed to stop as his gaze fell on the slow-moving ceiling fan. It appeared to be charred. Somewhat panicked but slightly relieved, he realized that it was covered in thick, smoke-colored fur from his cat! The pet sitter reported that Cashmere had scratched himself raw and pulled out a large patch of fur. She said that excessive shedding might be usual for Cashmere, but it definitely wasn't natural. She handed Jeff a bottle of Dream Coat, a healthy vitamin supplement she had just found at the health food store. (Dream Coat is my own blend of vegetable oils, but you can make it up at home yourself using the recipe below.)

At first, Jeff thought giving vitamins to a cat was a bit over-the-top; he figured Cashmere had to be getting everything he needed from his store-bought food. He even bragged that his mother fed the same kind of food to her cat, which lived to be seventeen. The sitter couldn't convince Jeff to change Cashmere's food, but since the hairy sofa had put such a kink in Jeff's social life, he decided to give the vitamins a try.

Supplementing with the oils took some getting used to, as both Jeff and his cat were creatures of habit. But after Jeff got the hang of it and Cashmere began to enjoy it, the furniture no longer needed covers. As Cashmere's health improved in many ways, Jeff opened up to trying out other holistic practices. He tossed out the old bagged kibble, discovered books on caring for pets naturally, and decided that he and Cashmere could both use a long overdue remodel. Jeff became a regular at the health food store and even took some organic cooking classes. He quickly became a believer and turned into one of those truly finicky pet owners, eagerly preparing Cashmere's meals every day. And Jeff has been happy to get back into hosting his black-tie parties at home now that both Cashmere and the furniture are proudly back on display.

This week, you'll start giving your pet the oil blend that turned things around for Cashmere. Here's the recipe.

RECIPE FOR A BEAUTIFUL COAT

Yield: 8 ounces

5 ounces soybean oil or olive oil

1 ounce cod liver oil

1 ounce wheat germ oil

1 ounce flaxseed oil

1 clove garlic, or 1 teaspoon garlic powder

2-inch sprig of rosemary, or $^1/_2$ teaspoon dried rosemary

Combine all of the ingredients in a blender or food processor and pulse for 30 seconds. Pour into a dark or opaque glass bottle or jar and seal tightly. Store in the refrigerator for freshness, where it will keep for about 2 months. Serving sizes are based on body weight; use the dosage recommended below and thoroughly mix it into your pet's food at every meal.

PET'S WEIGHT		AMOUNT OF EFA BLEND
2 to 11 pounds	—	$1/2$ teaspoon
12 to 25 pounds	—	1 teaspoon
26 to 50 pounds	—	2 teaspoons
51 to 100 pounds	—	1 tablespoon

Tips: You can double up the dosage to jump-start the effects initially, then drop down to maintenance levels after you've achieved results. Seasonal changes may dictate using more or less; let your senses guide you.

Tip for Cats: Some cats are creatures of habit and only like what you gave them yesterday. Most cats take to healthy supplements quickly, but if yours doesn't, start with just a few drops mixed thoroughly into its food on day one, then gradually increase the dosage over a week or two.

Caution: Light and heat can damage unsaturated fatty acids. That's why it's important to store the EFA blend in a cool, dark place. Storing it in glass is also important, as oil readily combines with most types of plastic to form toxic compounds.

A TEMPORARY SETBACK

Most pets respond to supplementation of EFAs with immediate improvement of the coat and skin, but others may go through a brief period where these initially seem to worsen. If this happens to your pet, don't worry; you're still on the right track. When a pet has been on a poor-quality diet without supplementation all its life, its body will have a multitude of toxins built up. Much like humans who embark on a new program of natural foods and supplements, it's not unusual for some pets to experience a brief period of detoxification before the actual healing begins to take place. This is commonly referred to as a "healing crisis." Since the skin is an amazing organ of elimination, you may notice a brief aggravation of symptoms. Relax. It's just the body doing its job of cleansing and healing the system. Even though your pet may appear to be scratching or shedding more, this generally subsides in a few days, and then you'll start to see improvement.

Some pets experience a change in just a few days; it may appear as a shine that wasn't there before, or a subtle change in hair or coat texture. Other pets may take up to a month or more before you notice the difference. Be patient. Your pet will respond favorably. It may have taken months or years of feeding the wrong foods for your pet to get to where it is, and a few more weeks should not be too long to wait. The good news is that I've never heard of anyone who didn't experience improvement.

Now let's delve into the healing properties and uses of the ingredients in my healing oil blend: soybean oil, cod liver oil, wheat germ oil, flaxseed oil, garlic, and rosemary.

SOYBEAN OIL

I love the endless health benefits that soybean oil provides for all pets. I think it's possibly one of the best oils around because it features omega-3 fatty acids and is the primary commercial source for vitamin E, which defends against forms of cell damage, ranging from cancers, heart disease, and cataracts to premature aging and arthritis. More specifically, liquid soybean oil has a very favorable fatty acid profile: it has zero trans fat, it's low in saturated fat ("bad fats"), and it's high in poly- and monounsaturated fats ("good fats"). This combination helps soybean oil lower the risk of heart disease not just for your pet, but for you as well.

Caution: The oil from soybeans provides a source of fat that's easy to assimilate when used in moderation and as a supplement. But there's another side of soy that can be dangerous when soybeans are used as a major protein source in pet foods. Because of bottom-line economics, soy and its derivatives, like soy meal, soy flour, soy grits, and isolated soy proteins, have become increasingly common in commercial pet foods because they're so cheap. But there is a hidden expense: the health of our pets. Soy has been recognized as one of the leading causes of bloat in dogs, a potentially fatal and always painful gastrointestinal problem. When soy is listed in the top six ingredients on a pet food label, you can bet that the manufacturer is not looking out for your best friend's health.

COD LIVER OIL

You may remember a time when your grandmother proclaimed that a spoonful of cod liver oil a day not only prevented disease, but could also cure pretty much anything. Well, she may have been right! I can't say enough good things about this oil either. It increases energy, enhances concentration, and helps prevent heart disease, cancer, and depression. It may well be the cure for the common cold, and it's probably better than a flu shot. Research also indicates it helps fight Alzheimer's, arthritis, and diabetes. The best kept pet breeder secret? It's excellent for pregnant pets, reducing premature births, low birth weight, and other complications. Cod liver oil is the best natural source of usable omega-3 fatty acids for pets, and most like the taste.

You can also use salmon oil, another potent fish oil, in place of cod liver oil. Make sure you choose an oil made from wild, open-water fish. Some products on the market are derived from farm-raised fish and therefore may contain harmful levels of heavy metals and contaminants that could slow down the healing process and stand in the way of results.

WHEAT GERM OIL

This rich source of vitamin E comes from the heart of the wheat berry and helps to repair cell membranes. Antioxidants in wheat germ oil help to stop free radicals from damaging nerve cells. It strengthens muscles, promotes healthy eye function, and improves vital organs such as the heart and the lungs.

FLAXSEED OIL

Sled dog owners give their huskies flaxseed oil to help sustain energy, strengthen bones, and heal chapped paws. It's full of powerful EFAs, which prevent cellular damage and have antiaging, anti-inflammatory, and antitumor properties (see chapter 8 for more on this topic). It's wonderful for the heart, helps lower cholesterol, lowers blood pressure, and helps with skin and coat problems. Be extremely careful about storing this oil properly, though. Flaxseed oil is very volatile and spoils more easily than any of the others. Get into the habit of performing an aroma check whenever you use it, and never use any oil that smells sour or rancid. Personally, I don't recommend flaxseed oil as a source of omega-3s for pets because they can't utilize the ALA it provides. But because its other properties are so valuable, it's still an important ingredient in my oil blend.

GARLIC

We all know garlic has numerous beneficial properties. It's used to treat everything from the common cold to cancer, but more importantly for pets, it stimulates digestion and boosts the immune system. It's rich in protein, vitamins A, B_1, and C, and essential minerals, including calcium, magnesium, potassium, iron, and selenium. It also contains seventeen different amino acids. When used in the right proportions it's a natural antibiotic, and it's recommended by every holistic veterinarian I know. Why? Because vampires aren't the only bloodsuckers this flavorful bulb repels. It helps control intestinal parasites, including tapeworms, roundworms, and hookworms, and repels the bane of some pets' existence—fleas. It's also an excellent antifungal agent.

> ### "Garlic helps to eliminate worms, strengthen digestion and beneficially stimulate the intestinal tract. It is also indicated for animals that tend to be overweight or suffer hip pain from arthritis or dysplasia."
>
> —RICHARD H. PITCAIRN, DVM, author of
> *Dr. Pitcairn's Complete Guide to Natural Health for Dogs and Cats*

ROSEMARY

An entire book could be written about the incredible healing properties of this aromatic, culinary herb; its uses are endless. It's long been used as a natural, soothing digestive aid and to relieve gas. The ancient Greeks believed it could enhance memory, and today's scientists are proving them right. Just a whiff can sharpen the brain and overcome

The Goodness of Garlic

I can't say enough great things about garlic; it's an extraordinary herb. Egyptians, Romans, and Israelis once thought it possessed magical powers for increasing stamina and strengthening the body. Herbalists have long claimed that garlic kills germs, expels worms, and destroys fungi, bacteria, and yeast. Holistic veterinarians are unanimous in the opinion that garlic is undeniably useful for animals; most have dubbed it "nature's antibiotic."

Garlic contains allicin, which is responsible for its strong aroma but also provides antibacterial action equivalent to that of 1 percent penicillin. Be aware that allicin isn't released until garlic is finely chopped or crushed, and the finer and more intensive the crushing, the stronger the medicinal effect. However, allicin starts breaking apart immediately after it's released. Cooking speeds this process up as well, and microwaving completely destroys allicin, thus removing most of the health benefits of garlic. Therefore, cold-pressed, virgin garlic oil is a great way to get all of garlic's healing nutrients, but it can be hard to find. Though it's not quite the same, you can make a version of garlic oil at home by placing a clove of garlic (whole or pressed) into a jar of oil, along with some rosemary to help preserve freshness.

This wondrous onion-like bulb boosts the immune system, purifies the blood, and supports healthy heart and lung function. It can be minced and roasted in a pan with butter, then added to foods to provide a mild, nutty flavor that dogs and cats really enjoy. The beneficial effects of garlic are too great to ignore, and it's also considered one of the safest herbs on the planet when used in moderation. In recent years there have been controversies about its safety, with claims that in large doses it can upset the digestive tract, but I've never witnessed any negative effects from garlic use. I always recommend giving pets garlic daily to keep their bodies strong and vibrant. I suggest a clove a day for a medium-sized dog and $2/3$ clove a day for cats.

Garlic Tip: Fresh, whole cloves of garlic are always best. Whole garlic should be stored in a cool, dry, dark place, but not in the refrigerator.

fatigue (so it's especially helpful for working or sporting dogs). This is due to rosemary's high concentration of antioxidants and its ability to help prevent the breakdown of the neurotransmitter acetylcholine. Rosemary is also beneficial for the heart, liver, and eyes, and it helps improve hair and coat quality and stimulates the appetite. Although rosemary oil is too strong for internal use other than in tiny quantities, it's great for aromatherapy; try sprinkling a few drops on potpourri.

Added Benefits of EFAs for Senior Pets

Like the Tin Man in *The Wizard of Oz*, senior pets need a good oiling to help with joint and heart health. Many health problems associated with EFA deficiencies are exacerbated as our pets age: susceptibility to infections, kidney degeneration, behavioral problems, liver diseases, arthritic conditions, heart and circulatory problems, and overall weakness. In short, lack of high-quality EFAs may be contributing to your pet's problem every bit as much as age.

How to Select High-Quality Oils

Selecting high-quality oils to use as supplements is easy: always choose extra-virgin, cold-pressed oils. Extra-virgin oils are the result of a single, simple pressing, and are characterized by perfect flavor and odor. These are the highest-quality oils. "Cold-pressed" refers to an extraction style: pressing and/or grinding at low temperatures. Oils that are cold-pressed retain all of their flavor, aroma, and nutritional value.

If you don't want to make your own blend using the recipe on page 76, then look for a blend of oils that contains wheat germ, sunflower, safflower, soy, and cod liver oils. Most health food stores or finer pet stores offer a selection of products to choose from. Make sure the oil is packaged in a dark-colored, glass bottle. High-quality oils are never packaged in clear or plastic containers because direct sunlight (and heat) can damage them.

When it comes to problem solving, we know that two heads are better than one, and the same applies to combining oils. A blend of essential oils works best to promote health for dogs and cats because each oil has a different nutritional profile, and each provides things that the others don't. If you add only one type of oil to your pet's food, you won't see the same health benefits that four or more oils will achieve.

Week One Assessment

You and your pet have completed the first week of the eight-week program. Congratulations on getting started! Now it's time to look at what you've accomplished. Read through the assessment questions below and record in your journal what happened during the week and where you and your pet are now.

❏   Did you identify the pet foods in your pantry that may contain questionable ingredients?

❏   Did you tune in to pet food companies' various marketing ploys and raise your consciousness about how advertising agencies dominate our perceptions with claims that are often counter to the reality? How many commercial pet foods claim they'll make your pet healthy? How many of them have you actually tried on your pet? How many of them have you wondering?

❏   Does your pet exhibit signs of any skin and coat problems, such as shedding, itching, scratching, and the like? If so, how big of a problem is it and where are the areas of greatest concern? Get ready to make this a thing of the past.

❏   Did you add essential fatty acids to your pet's diet? If so, what oils did you use and how often did you supplement? Adding oils brings balance to a previously dried-out system; have you witnessed any results yet? (With smaller pets, you may even see results overnight.)

❑ Did your pet experience a brief aggravation of any symptoms, such as more shedding or scratching? This should not deter you. Your pet's body is healing and after a few days, should respond in a positive way.

Daily Play

How have those daily play dates been going? Take ten minutes a day, every day, and if you feel like playing more, go for it! Here are some fun ideas for play with your pet.

Cat Play Tip: Create an obstacle course by placing five or six plastic drinking cups in a zigzag row along the floor. Encourage your cat to weave in and out of them by dangling a string or a feather and pulling it through the obstacle course as they chase it. The object of the game is to get your pet to move and to stimulate its body and its mind.

Dog Play Tip: Your dog feeds on your feelings, so always have a positive attitude when playing with your dog. It's important for your dog to be comfortable during play sessions.

◆ ◆ ◆

You've learned about the nourishing power of EFAs, what they can do for your pet, and how to choose them, combine them, and add them to your pet's diet. You've been using my Recipe for a Beautiful Coat and should be seeing some results. This week's study of the pet foods in your cupboard—particularly the dry foods—and the marketing pitches used to sell them should have you eager to take the next step.

In week two, you'll jettison the harmful commercial foods and replace them with your own home-cooked healthy stews and other hearty main-meal recipes, with a range of tasty toppings to ease your pet into the new diet. And be sure to keep using the EFAs in your pet's diet! For the next seven weeks, the program will build in this way—each week adding vital new components of the Whole Pet Plan, so by the end of week eight you will have incorporated all of them.

CHAPTER FOUR

Week Two:
The Art of the Stew

In your journal:

- Complete the Weekly Checkup.

- Schedule your daily play dates.

- Throughout the week, fill in the Week at a Glance.

- At week's end, complete the Weekly Assessment.

Last week, we made it a point to observe, research, study, and reflect. You became aware of what's in your pantry and paid attention to the actual ingredients in the food you've been feeding your pet. This week it's time for a big change: you're going to clean out that pantry. You'll stock up with fresh ingredients, instead, to make the same stew that turned things around for my cat Spot and started me on this path. There are other recipes to try and feeding tips for cats and for dogs. Some of the recommended foods may surprise you. Others, like Seafood Gumbo, Burger Stew, and Turkey Tetrazzini, will show you I'm serious when I say pets should eat as well as people! You'll also learn about tasty additions to ease the transition for your pet and boost its digestion.

What to Expect

A happy eater, as well as a greater sense of well-being for both you and your pet. Most pets take to their new fare right away, but if you have a dry food addict or are working with a creature of habit, feel free to incorporate bribe foods (see chapter 5 for ideas) and use them liberally to get your pet started. This transition period may be difficult for you, too. It's natural to feel some doubt, or even a little guilt, when imposing such big changes on your dog or cat. Remember that you're doing this for your pet's health, and try to keep a positive attitude at all times. Soon your pet's body will begin to change with the healthier food, giving you signs that you're on the right track to help your pet with weight problems, lower its risk of diseases, and increase its body's own natural ability to heal. Vomiting, digestive disorders, and bowel problems will probably become a thing of the past this week. Notice every aspect of your pet's health improve as real, wholesome, fresh foods help strengthen and rejuvenate its body.

Project: Out with the Old, In with the New

It's time to toss out anything and everything with pet-grade ingredients: fillers (such as corn, wheat, rice, or potato), by-products, chemicals, preservatives, sugars, salts, or coloring agents. That means all commercial foods, canned, dry, or otherwise. Grab a garbage bag, toss everything in it, and go directly to the dumpster. If you can't bear to throw it away, you could donate it; many shelters are desperate for food of any kind. However, tossing it out is a cathartic act that says you're making room for a healthier way of life. (But before tossing anything out, please think about the environment and take the time to empty and recycle containers such as cans and cardboard boxes.) Remember, you're clearing out your pantry so you can clean out your pet. You're getting rid of poor-quality products that are bad for your pet's health, and thus bad for you. You're breaking away from old habits, so don't hold back. Remember, this is not a short-term plan; this is a new way of life.

Now don your apron and grab a wooden spoon. You're about to create a culinary masterpiece so colorful and full of life that your friends may mistake you for a five-star celebrity chef. This week, you'll witness the miracle of real food and learn what it means to the health and longevity of your pet. We'll look carefully at the ingredients of a healthy homemade stew and discover what Grandma knew all along about the healing power of chicken and vegetable broth: it's good for the immune system, has anti-inflammatory properties, and is the best natural remedy for repairing a wide array of medical problems. I'll explain the why and how of making your own pet food and using it to build a strong foundation for your pet's health.

The Life Blood

The basis for the Whole Pet Diet is healthy, homemade stews. The first layer of this culinary art form is the nutrient-rich broth. We'll enhance this foundation by adding lots of high-quality ingredients to enhance every aspect of your pet's being. The recipes in this chapter are specifically designed to replicate as closely as possible what an animal eats in the wild. Enhanced digestion and absorption of important vitamins and minerals are just two of the many benefits of these stews.

THE SECRET IS IN THE BROTH

Feeding your pet vitamin- and mineral-rich chicken and vegetable broth is one of the simplest and least expensive ways to improve its digestion and overall health. Cooked slowly over low heat, the stew's broth captures important minerals and antioxidants from organic or natural meats and vegetables. Use human-grade ingredients, and if your budget allows, it's best to choose organic ingredients. Always use a wide variety of differently colored vegetables; this is one of the best ways to bring the body's pH into balance. An acid pH level in the body is the beginning of many chronic diseases, and is the most common pH imbalance. To help with acidity, the stew creates an alkaline pH level in the body with the help of carrots, zucchini, a pinch of garlic, and a little sea kelp.

A naturally enriched broth of this kind is especially important for overstressed cats and dogs who have been fed commercial pet foods containing too many chemicals, grains, and sugars. These unfortunate critters are most likely dehydrated and depleted of valuable minerals and can become dangerously overacidic. Even kittens and puppies get depleted, and when they do, digestion fails; the liver, spleen, and pancreas become weak; and the bones and joints can develop osteoporosis, arthritis, and other diseases. My recipe for chicken and vegetable broth is naturally full of proteins, vitamins, and minerals, and it brings acidity and alkalinity back into balance. Because every ingredient used is easy to digest, your pet's body doesn't have to expend excess energy on the digestion process and can save it for healing.

Hydration is key. Your pet's body is made up of about 75 percent water. Out in the wild it would be consuming prey—a bird, mouse, lizard, or rabbit whose body is also made up of about 75 percent water. At less than 10 percent moisture, dry foods couldn't be any more unnatural. When your pet eats kibble, it's missing out on a lot of the water it should get from its diet. In order to compensate for a dry diet, pets would have to drink unnatural amounts of water just to flush out toxins, hydrate organs, and aid in elimination.

BASIC INGREDIENTS FOR A MAGICAL HEALING STEW

The restorative and preventive health benefits of home-cooked stews are widely acknowledged and steeped in tradition. Every culture has a favorite stew, and every cook a secret ingredient. The beauty of this much-loved, one-pot meal is that it can be made using just about any meat as the base. The better the quality of ingredients, the better the stew flavor and results. Be sure to use choice cuts of meat, and don't forget about beneficial organ meats; these can be easily added to stews and can result in some outstanding functional improvements (I'll get into this later).

ABOUT THE PREPARATION

Cooking is a labor of love, and it's important to prepare and handle the food for your pet as carefully as you would for any other member of your family (believe me, when they smell it cooking, they may try to sneak a bowl behind your back!) Begin with clean utensils and a clean, organized work area. Wash your hands before and during food preparation. Ideally, you'd begin simmering your stew as soon as you arrive home with your "fresh kill" from the butcher, adding organically grown vegetables from your garden. But in the real world, you might have to buy your vegetables at the store, too. It's just as important to ensure food safety for your pet as it is for your family, so keep the meat in the refrigerator until you're ready to add it to the pot, and always defrost meat or poultry completely in the refrigerator before using it.

Eating habits are as varied for pets as they are for humans. An active, growing, or working pet will require more food than its sedentary cousin. Many pets eat more in the winter than they do in the summer.

Cooking and Feeding Tips

Time-Saving Tip: Although fresh vegetables contain more nutrients, it's fine to keep a few bags of organic frozen, diced vegetables in the freezer to help cut prep time when you're pressed for time.

For Cats: Cats should be allowed to eat for thirty minutes twice daily. This gives the body plenty of time for brief fasts throughout the day. Remove and clean up all uneaten food after the thirty minutes is up.

For Dogs: To stretch meals for dogs, you can add a slice or two of sprouted whole-grain bread to each meal upon serving. Just chop it up coarsely and mix it right in.

For Ailing Pets: A pet that's under the weather and or in recovery should start with broth only. It will be easier for it to process this rich fluid filled with amino acids. And since its body won't have to expend any extra effort in the digestion process, this leaves more energy for healing.

Important Cautions for All Pets: Never serve hot or cold food to your pet; room temperature is best. Never serve cooked chicken bones to a pet; they splinter easily and can become lodged in the throat or digestive tract.

SPOT'S CHICKEN STEW

Yield: 20 cups / Serving Size: See below

2^1/$_2$ pounds whole chicken or turkey (bones, organs, skin, and all)

^{1}/$_4$ cup chopped fresh garlic

1 cup green peas

1 cup coarsely chopped carrots

^{1}/$_2$ cup coarsely chopped sweet potato

^{1}/$_2$ cup coarsely chopped zucchini

^{1}/$_2$ cup coarsely chopped yellow squash

^{1}/$_2$ cup coarsely chopped green beans

^{1}/$_2$ cup coarsely chopped celery

1 tablespoon kelp powder

1 tablespoon dried rosemary

11 to 16 cups springwater

For dogs only: Add 8 ounces whole barley and 6 ounces rolled oats, and adjust the water content to a total of 16 cups or enough to cover the ingredients (I don't recommend the grains portions for cats).

Combine all of the ingredients in a 10-quart stockpot (stainless steel, please) with enough water to cover. Bring to a boil, then turn down the heat as low as possible and simmer for 2 hours (the carrots should be quite soft at the end of the cooking time). Remove from the heat, let cool, and debone the chicken. With an electric hand mixer, or using a food processor and working in batches, blend all the ingredients into a nice puree; the stew should be slightly thicker for dogs and more soupy for cats. Using ziplock bags or plastic yogurt containers, make up meal-sized portions. Refrigerate what you'll need for three days and freeze the rest. Be sure and seek your pet's advice on ideal meal sizes.

Serving Size: Amounts will vary depending on age, activity level, current health, weight, and season, but here are some guidelines. The average adult cat will eat roughly 1 cup a day. Because dogs vary so much in size, consult the table below. The amount shown should be split into at least two meals daily.

DOG'S WEIGHT	TOTAL DAILY PORTION
Up to 10 pounds	1 to 1^1/$_2$ cups
11 to 20 pounds	2 to 3 cups
21 to 40 pounds	4 cups

For each additional 20 pounds, add 2 cups. Remember, all pets are individuals, so let your intuition and observations guide you.

Monitor your pet's weight and energy levels in your journal on a weekly basis to help you determine optimum serving size. Some pets may greedily gobble up this new diet, while others may be less impressed with their new fare. It will take a few days of trial feedings to figure out what's perfectly appropriate for your pet.

My six-year-old, slow-moving male cat, Kitty, will eat about one cup a day, while his more active two-year-old sister, Bijoux, chows down on nearly two cups in a sitting. This makes sense, because Bijoux climbs trees, chases lizards, and gets into everything, whereas Kitty's favorite activity is sleeping on my puffy pillow. During stressful times, both cats eat less. Pay attention, observe, and listen to your pets. They have much to teach us.

Let's meet another real pet that got a new lease on life with homemade chicken stew. Some "back from the brink" stories seem like miracles, while others make perfect sense. This one is a bit of both.

The Miracle Valentine Gift

I first had the pleasure of meeting the lovely Ms. Valen when Judy decided to bring her indoors and put a stop to her freewheeling days along Clearwater Beach. Valen was a seventeen-year-old calico kitty with the sweetest disposition and a purr so loud it could wake up the neighbors. Valen's original family had just gotten bad news: the elderly cat had developed feline lower urinary tract disease (FLUTD), which meant her kidneys were failing, and she had also developed cancer. They were told she only had weeks to live and that at this late stage of her life the kind thing to do was to put her to sleep. But Judy had grown too fond of this special cat to give up their ritual of watching the sunset on the beach together, and she somehow felt that it just wasn't Valen's time.

Poor Valen was feeling so bad at this point that she had simply stopped eating and took to hiding in the closet. Her painful and frequent trips to the litter box, where she was unable to relieve her bladder, were as miserable for Judy as they were for her Valen. Sadly, far too many cats succumb to this potentially deadly disease, but Judy believed in her heart that it was no death sentence. I urged her to read as much as she could about kidney failure in Anitra Frazier's The New Natural Cat, *and Judy was as eager a student as I have ever known.*

Judy had observed my work with animals and had seen for herself that so many pets had been healed, often with a simple change in lifestyle. Because Judy was inclined toward alternative health herself, my suggestions of homemade food, herbs, and homeopathic preparations fit nicely with her belief system.

Patience and determination paid off. Valen began to eat her homemade, healthy chicken broth and regained some much-needed energy. I suggested using only the broth to quickly boost Valen's strength without taxing her already stressed digestive system. As her entire body began to heal, so did her kidneys. Her trips to the litter box became less frequent, and she no longer strained to urinate. Once she appeared more stable, solid pieces of the chicken stew were added to her daily fare, along with various vitamin supplements to support her body in fighting her cancer. I also recommended a holistic vet, who chose a specific homeopathic remedy for her particular symptoms, and Judy used an eyedropper to give Valen daily infusions of horsetail grass tea. This approach worked, as Valen obviously felt better with each passing day.

To this day, I firmly believe there is nothing about the body that cannot be improved or changed when it's given the right nutritional support. Beautiful Valen went on to live another eleven years after I met her, which made her twenty-eight years old when she finally passed away. Judy was right. She instinctively knew that they had another lifetime of sunsets to share.

I am joyful that I have been a part of keeping many more pets alive, healthy, and vibrant, even after an owner is told there is nothing that can be done. We are only limited by our own knowledge, or lack thereof. True love is always a wise love.

Now let's talk about what goes into my stew recipes, and why. I've studied the natural lifestyle of dogs and cats to determine the ratio of meat, vegetables, and grains appropriate for each. Omnivorous canines naturally eat a wide variety of foods, not just meat, and carnivorous felines invariably consume at least a bit of vegetable matter by eating herbivores (plant eaters). One way or another, Mother Nature sees to it that her all-important greens are consumed and utilized in animals' diets. For optimum health, holistic veterinarians suggest a cat's diet be made up of 60 percent meat and 40 percent veggies. This balances the digestive tract to help felines find their perfect weight. A dog's diet, on the other hand, is best composed of 40 percent meat, 50 percent veggies, and 10 percent grain or other carbohydrate. I've found that these ratios work well to assure the most fit and trim canines.

Getting Back to the Roots

Root vegetables are integral to any stew, not only for the delicious flavor they provide, but for their remarkable healing properties. Holistic health practitioners maintain that root vegetables provide stabilizing energy that focuses the brain and strengthens the will. Because these plants grow underground and are rich in minerals, vitamins, and other vital nutrients, they top the list of vegetables recommended in the treatment of cancers. Most dogs and cats enjoy carrots and sweet potatoes, and I recommend these two root vegetables be staple items in every stew you make.

Carrots contain abundant amounts of the antioxidant beta-carotene. According to Chinese medicine, carrots also contain an essential oil that kills parasites and unhealthy intestinal bacteria. Filled with silicon, this bright, colorful root helps the body metabolize calcium and strengthens connective tissues. Carrots are good for the eyes, ears, skin, and lungs.

Sweet potatoes are also highly nutritious, especially when the skin is consumed. They're rich in vitamin C, potassium, magnesium, niacin, thiamine, complex carbohydrates, and dietary fiber. They tone and firm internal organs, such as the spleen and pancreas, and are said to keep the kidney, stomach, and intestines in harmony because they contain some carbohydrates already in the form of simple sugars. They're a staple food of many cultures, and food scientists consider them to be highly nourishing.

Yams (and their cousin the sweet potato) are a rich source of vitamin A. I can't say enough about the importance of including them in a pet's diet. They're good for energy, inflammation, the kidneys, the spleen, and the pancreas, and they help remove toxins. They are also important for pregnant or lactating females and pets with diarrhea.

Above-Ground Veggies

Celery is another "must include" vegetable for your stew. Like carrots, they aid in digestion, but they also have cooling properties that help with inflammation, liver health, and urinary tract infections. Because celery is very high in silicon, it's good for bones, joints, and connective tissues. Both Eastern and Western medicinal diets recommend it for high blood pressure, and it's an amazing yet gentle diuretic.

Squash, another rich source of vitamin A, improves circulation, and its seeds help destroy parasitic worms. Choose either summer squash, or winter squash, as long as they are tender. Pumpkins are another form of squash, and their seeds also help eliminate worms. Pumpkin helps to balance the pancreas, which produces insulin, so it's especially important in the diets of pets with diabetes or hypoglycemia.

Green beans contain vitamin C and provide iron, vitamins, minerals, and dietary fiber. They're great for the spleen, pancreas, and kidneys.

Green peas are packed with goodness: vitamin C, folic acid, thiamine, niacin, iron, zinc, and protein. Peas are important to digestion in that they reduce vomiting, hiccups, gas, and coughing.

The Meat of the Matter

When it comes to meat, it's best to consider using sources that are down your pet's actual food chain. Let's face it; your ten-pound cat isn't likely to take down a five-hundred-pound cow. Animals that hunt typically eat animals that are smaller or weaker than they are. Lamb or beef may be substituted (or added) for the meat portions of your pet's stew, but they should be used sparingly for dogs, and as seldom as possible for cats.

I like fowl as the main component of stew because it's the easiest meat for your pet to digest. Lean chicken and turkey are easy for the body to process, especially if your dog or cat is having any health issues. The more difficult food is to digest, the more energy the body expends processing it.

Seafood is also a good choice. I think the best fish for feeding to pets are squid, sardines, and fresh anchovies (without added salt or preservatives); these are more pure and easier to find from wild sources. Small fish can be ground up, bones and all, and added to the stew. Just be sure to remove the gills and the contents of the gut. Wild salmon is great too, but I don't recommend using other large fish on a regular basis. Seafood is loaded with protein, minerals, and enzymes when fresh. It also has lots of collagen, and clams (in moderation) are an amazing source of taurine, an essential nutrient for cats (see page 98).

As you'll recall from week one, supplementing blended oils provides better nutrition than you'd get by supplementing just one, and the same holds true for most food groups. A well-fed pet needs to eat a variety of foods to get a wide variety and good balance of vitamins and minerals. So it's a good idea to alternate seafood stews with poultry stews, serving seafood about one to three times a week.

WHY ORGANIC MEAT?

As explained, the natural diet of canines and felines contains a high percentage of meat. One of the downsides of meat consumption for anyone, human or animal, is that toxins tend to become more concentrated higher up the food chain. You probably recall why DDT was banned in this country: this toxic compound, present in only minute amounts in plants, accumulated in such high concentrations in predatory birds that it caused nesting failures. This same sort of dynamic plays out with all sorts of environmental toxins. If your budget allows, always opt for organic or natural sources, when buying meat for yourself or your pet.

ORGANS FEED ORGANS

As unappetizing as organ meats may be to the American, human palate, in the wild your pet wouldn't skip its prey's liver, heart, or kidneys. When your pet doesn't get organ meats in its diet, it can miss out on significant concentrations of B vitamins and other nutrients and thus become anemic and not perform at its best. I believe that organs feed organs: heart feeds heart, liver feeds liver, and so on. To determine how much organ meat to use when you cook for your pet, add the same amount that would be found in the live prey. Don't worry, I've done the dirty work for you; the amount of organ meat is about one-sixth.

RAW VERSUS COOKED

Raw versus cooked foods is a controversial topic. Raw foods, particularly chicken and organ meat, carry all the contaminants and entail all the warnings for pets as they do for humans. The conventional veterinary community is rather leery about feeding raw foods, and holistic practitioners seem split in their opinions. Ann Martin, author of the chilling book *Foods Pets Die For*, warns against the use of raw foods entirely. After consulting with dozens of experts in the field of toxicology, she proclaims that raw food diets can contain devastating amounts of E coli and salmonella and that freezing can't kill these bacteria. She explains that laboratories actually preserve strains of bacteria and viruses by freezing them and maintains that cooking is the best way to eliminate the potential for illness.

I have my own theory and ideas about raw food diets. It's exceedingly difficult to duplicate a plate full of pulsating prey, or an animal's biological processes during the heat of the hunt. The thrill of the chase accelerates salivation, heart rate, and blood flow. Smell, too, helps ready the body for digestion. In the wild, there are long stretches or natural fasts between hunts, and during this time nature helps rid the body of toxins and prepare it for its next meal. These systems aid a wild animal's digestive process. It's highly doubtful that any companion animal has had to go very long between meals, or that it's revved up its motor before diving into a recently thawed fillet. No animal in the wild has a tidy dish of mouse waiting for it either, and many household pets may not get much exercise beyond strolling to the food bowl for a nibble every now and then. Let your dog trap a rabbit in the woods, or allow your cat to corner that lizard when the opportunity presents itself, but day in, day out, I recommend a cooked meat and vegetable stew supplemented with vitamins and carefully selected, safe raw foods to simulate the natural diet.

BUT I'M VEGETARIAN!

If you're vegetarian, you may have qualms about handling meat for your pet, and you may be wondering whether you can feed them a vegetarian diet. Cats need meat and without it, they can go blind. And while it is possible for dogs to be vegetarian, it's neither natural nor optimally healthful. Plus, you have to be very careful to ensure that a vegetarian dog gets all the nutrients it needs in the right proportions.

Look at it this way: you probably chose to be vegetarian, at least in part, because of a holistic orientation. If you look at your pet holistically, too, you must understand that its metabolism and dietary requirements are quite different than yours, and that meat is an important and natural part of its diet. Since you're conscious of the importance of whole foods for yourself, you already understand how this relates to your pets. Unfortunately, most commercial pet foods don't offer anything close to a pet's optimum diet. There are a few better-quality pet foods on the market these days, so if you can't bear to handle the meat, please take the time to seek these out and be willing to pay a bit more for them. Look for products with formulations similar to those in my recipes, but watch out for the ones that contain by-products (meat meals) and grains, or claim to be "made with organic ingredients." Read labels carefully, as they might use some organic grains, but their meat could be far from healthy.

By making and designing your pet's food, you can serve up feasts that are as healthful and loving for your pet as your own meals are for you. Since you've chosen to live with a carnivorous companion, be honest about your pet's needs. If this quandary haunts you, next time you're adding a pet to the family, consider a bird, rabbit, guinea pig, or other herbivore. These animals can make delightful friends, too, and might be more in keeping with your beliefs.

CATS NEED THEIR TAURINE

One final note while we're discussing meat: taurine is an essential nutrient for cats and critical to their immune system response. This amino acid is involved in many of their metabolic processes and is important for good vision, a healthy heart, and an active, engaged brain. Among humans, taurine is also known to be helpful in the treatment of epilepsy and hyperactivity. Good natural sources of taurine are high-quality muscle and organ meat, including beef, lamb, chicken, clams, oysters, and codfish. My favorite source of taurine is clams. They taste great, they're affordable, and cats love them. But be sure to use shellfish sparingly, as it's not as easy to assimilate as fowl.

Good Grains and Bad Grains

Grains can be a healthy source of long-term energy and energy storage for dogs. However, cats don't tolerate grain well at all; it tends to make their urine more alkaline and can cause feline lower urinary tract disease (FLUTD). These true carnivores are better served with a high-quality meat and vegetable diet.

Even for dogs, grains can also be bag or can fillers that lead to dangerous ailments like obesity and diabetes. You may recall from the introduction that corn, the number one filler in most commercial foods, is essentially indigestible for pets. Quinoa (pronounced keen-wa) and oatmeal are the best grains to incorporate into your dog's meals. Any grain you feed to your dog should be used in whole form so that it supplies more fiber and vitamins and minerals. Refined grains have most of their bran and nutrient-rich germ removed and therefore provide little or no nutritional or dietary benefit.

It gets a little confusing; even my once-favorite whole-grain bagel proved to be anything but, and it surprised me to learn that unbleached wheat flour is, in fact, essentially the same as white flour. If you want to add a slice of whole-grain bread to your dog's stew, make sure it's made with grains from the list below.

- Rolled oats are highly nutritious and high in cholesterol-fighting soluble fiber.

- Barley is high in fiber, it's easy to digest, and it's pleasing to most dogs' palates.

- Quinoa is a nutritionally superb grain. It provides complete protein and is an excellent source of B vitamins and magnesium.

- Millet is considered to be one of the least allergenic and most digestible grains. Plus, it's warming, so it will help heat your dog's body in cold or rainy seasons.

- Brown rice is a highly nutritious, nutty whole grain. When used in an appropriate proportion, it's an excellent addition to any dog's stew.

Please note, however, that diabetic dogs do much better without grains in their diet. The excess production of insulin that results from consuming grains only belabors their already troubled systems and can also lead to obesity. I believe the high corn and rice content in many commercial pet foods is the reason so many cats and dogs are overweight, and that this is also responsible for the growing incidence of diabetes, faulty metabolism, and problematic blood sugar levels among pets.

Putting Your Paw Down

By now you should be fully convinced of the nourishing power of our meat and vegetable stew (with small amounts of whole grains for your dog). But how will your pet feel about the change?

Some pets are a little reluctant to change foods, or even behavior patterns. In regard to supplements and foods, it can be even harder because their commercial foods contain addictive ingredients like sugars, salts, and flavor enhancers. Cats particularly demonstrate this behavior; I liken them to children who enjoy that hot dog and bag of chips for lunch every single day. It might be tasty, but it's just not healthy!

Your pet can't read, and it relies on your emotions. So make sure you convey your enthusiasm even if what it sees is a bowlful of strangeness. This new food smells different, looks different, and tastes different. Though some pets will dig right in without coaxing, with others it can be a challenge to change to healthier eating. The answer is to be firm. I call it "putting your paw down." Though it may be difficult at first, in the long run the benefits of making the switch will far outweigh the difficulties. Keep the goal in mind: the happiness and longevity of your beloved companion. If you're still worried, rest assured; in over twenty years I've never seen a single case of a healthy pet actually starving itself when given the opportunity to eat real food. Be firm. Forge on!

Another aspect of putting your paw down is switching diets cold turkey. In my early years, I pussyfooted around and encouraged people to add the new food or supplement into the old food and do a slower change. But for the last ten years, I've encouraged people to jump right in. I decided this approach was best for two reasons. First, when you make the change gradually, it generally takes longer to make the switch. So if you're not strong enough to be firm in your convictions, it could lead to giving up and going back to the old food; then everyone loses. Second, since every pet can and will make the switch (especially with the addition of bribe foods, which I'll get to in a minute), the more quickly you make the change, the more quickly the health benefits will start to show up. This makes the process more rewarding and satisfying for everyone involved. But to smooth the experience, you do have my permission to bribe your pet—especially if it's a cat.

Bribes

Many cats are creatures of habit. I purposely steer away from using the term *finicky* because it implies cats are just that way forever and cannot be changed—like they were born with some sort of "finicky" gene. Habits can be changed, and a creature of habit has a chance of changing or learning a new, healthier habit. It may take a little work, but pets can be weaned away from dangerously addictive commercial foods by using bribes—treats offered to entice a pet to eat healthier. My experience has been that when cat owners switch to feeding healthier food, about half of the cats take to the new food immediately. The other half often look at the food, then caterwaul around the kitchen demanding their old food or simply walk away uninterested. Particularly reticent and expressive cats may try to bury the food. My bribes are fine for all cats, but they're specifically designed for the unwilling half.

The most well-known but ill-used bribe food is tuna fish. I recommend against using tuna because it contains high levels of mercury, as well as mineral salts that can form into urinary crystals and lead to urinary tract infections. It also robs the body of vitamin E and creates addictions. Read the sidebar Mother's Little Helpers for ideas for natural and healthy treats to use as bribes. And if you need yet more ideas for treats, don't despair; week three is entirely devoted to the art of the treat.

As I explained in chapter 2, adult pets in good health should be fed twice a day and their bowls removed between meals, allowing cats up to thirty minutes to finish at their own pace. For dogs, follow the guidelines on serving size provided with the stew recipe on page 90, and be careful not to confuse your pet's enthusiasm for eating delicious, healthy food with hunger. If your pet gobbles up its new food with unusual gusto, don't jump to the conclusion that it is so ravenous it needs a second helping. It's more likely that you've stimulated its appetite with

Mother's Little Helpers: Treats as Bribes

If your pet is reluctant to make the switch to its new diet, sometimes a little something extra will coax it to the food bowl. Think of these bribes as tasty condiments to add some zing to its meal! The functional foods listed below can entice your pet, but most of them are also healthful and serve as supplements, providing extra vitamins, proteins, or other nutrients. A heartier cat will love the meats, eggs, and cheeses, while a cat under the weather will greatly appreciate the eggs, olive oil, or yogurt.

> Meat slivers (chicken, turkey, beef, lamb, or fish; avoid pork and tuna products)
>
> A few small pieces of cooked organic liver
>
> A few drops of natural tamari
>
> A few shakes of natural Parmesan cheese
>
> A dollop of tomato sauce
>
> A teaspoon of organic plain yogurt
>
> A spoonful of oil from a jar of olives
>
> A finely chopped olive
>
> A dollop of cottage cheese
>
> A dollop of meat-based baby food
>
> Raw or soft-boiled egg

Try mixing a bit of any of the above bribe foods into the new food or sprinkling it on top. Sometimes an irresistible condiment is all it takes to get a reluctant pet revved up and excited about the new fare. If there's something you know your cat is wild about, get creative and use just a little bit to get it going. Dogs don't usually need any coaxing to try the new meals, but any of the bribe foods can be used for dogs, as well.

your delicious, healthy stew. Stick with the recommended portions for your pet's weight. For a sick or recovering pet it's fine to offer a smaller second helping for the first few days. Keep an eye on your pet for any weight gain or loss and adjust its food intake accordingly. Remember, you're the caregiver, and every pet has different needs—needs that are continuously changing according to circumstances and current health levels.

Add Tasty Toppings to Boost Digestion

When you prepare food for your pet, mix in some healthy and tasty toppings loaded with live enzymes to help with digestion. Voyko adds freshly crushed garlic, parsley, kelp, and a spoonful or two of mashed papaya or pineapple. Live enzymes (found in the papaya and pineapple) are extremely important because they help the body digest and absorb vital nutrients in food. This is especially important if your pet isn't eating as much as normal when you change its food. The following toppers not only add delicious flavor, but each brings its own natural healing advantage to the mix:

- Garlic, the cure-all remedy mentioned in week one, tastes great, boosts the immune system, and has antibiotic and antiviral properties.

- Kelp is loaded with minerals, helps remove heavy metals, aids in digestion, and benefits the kidneys. These delicious sea vegetables are natural fungicides, and according to Asian medicine they're good for the heart, lungs, thyroid, and breath.

- Papaya, when under-ripe and complete with seeds, is filled with papain, a digestive enzyme that helps break down protein and eliminates plaque on the teeth. Papaya is also used in the diet to fight cancer and tumors.

- Pineapple, ripe and juicy, hydrates the body, destroys worms, and alleviates diarrhea. It's also great for digestion.

- Fresh parsley is an excellent topper for any pet meal (1 finely chopped teaspoon for medium-sized dogs and $1/2$ teaspoon for cats). It's one of the best sources of vitamin C, and provides vitamin A, calcium, magnesium, and iron. It's great for the teeth, it fights bad breath, and it can help prevent cancer. It's also purported to be effective for relieving ear infections and earaches and strengthening the optic and brain nerves, the adrenal glands, the gallbladder, and the kidneys.

Yogurt for Pets? Yes!

Now for a food that may surprise you but that's definitely recommended for your Whole Pet Diet: yogurt. It's such an excellent food that it deserves its own discussion. Mireille Guiliano, author of *French Women Don't Get Fat,* calls it a secret weapon, and the conqueror Genghis Kanh certainly agreed; he fortified his armies with it in the thirteenth century. Bulgarians, Turks, Tibetans, Greeks, Arabs, Indians, and Russians all credit their longevity to this sour, fermented food.

Even though dairy products generally aren't appropriate for dogs and cats (pasteurized dairy products are difficult to break down), yogurt is an exception. If you choose a yogurt with live cultures, its beneficial bacteria make it both more healthful and more easily digested by both dogs and cats. Yogurt is a good source of calcium in a form that's readily absorbed in the body. It lowers cholesterol, boosts the immune system, and kills the bacteria that can cause ulcers and gastritis. According to a recent USDA report, yogurt with probiotic cultures (live yogurt) has even been proven to actually combat deadly salmonella bacteria. It has also been reported that yogurt promotes fat loss, especially around the tummy, and it aids in the retention of lean muscle mass. I love a midday snack of yogurt, and it's something I can feel good about sharing with any of my pets.

Yogurt may be made with the milk from cows, goats, sheep, mares, and now even water buffalo, and any of these are fine. What's important is that it be raw, unsweetened, plain, and unpasteurized; this ensures that the lactic-acid producing bacteria in the yogurt are alive and that they find their way to your pet's stomach, where they manufacture B vitamins and support or create healthy intestinal flora.

Although antibiotics may sometimes be necessary for your pet, they destroy all bacteria in the system, both good and bad, and greatly disturb the balance of the intestinal flora, which includes both beneficial and harmful bacteria. Therefore, while a pet is taking antibiotics, and for a week or two after the medicine is finished, it's critically important to feed it small amounts of yogurt to make sure it has sufficient levels of healthy bacteria in its digestive tract. This can remedy many digestive disorders, including diarrhea, and also combat yeast infections.

Yogurt can be a powerful tool in cleansing the intestinal tract of accumulated toxins. Practitioners of Chinese and Ayurvedic medicine consider undigested, unabsorbed, and unassimilated food to be toxins and the root of all disease. Because the intestinal tract assimilates most of the body's critical nutrients, these practitioners consider careful cleansing of this system to be paramount to health and longevity.

If you don't have time to make your own yogurt, I suggest buying an organic, unsweetened, cream-on-top variety. But there's nothing quite like fresh yogurt you've made yourself.

HOMEMADE YOGURT

Yield: 1 quart of yogurt / Serving Size: 1 tablespoon

1 quart organic whole cow's or goat's milk

1 cup plain organic yogurt (live culture)

Bring the milk to a full boil. Let it rise to the top of the pot, but don't let it boil over. Lower the heat and simmer until the milk reaches 110°F, stirring frequently so a skin doesn't form on top. Mix 1 cup of the warm milk with the yogurt. Pour this mixture back into the pot of warm milk and mix well. Pour into a glass bowl and cover (I usually use a clean kitchen towel). Keep the yogurt in a warm place (from 110°F to 120°F). A pilot light in the oven will usually keep it warm enough. Let the yogurt set for 6 to 8 hours, then store it in the refrigerator, where it will keep for about a week. Bring each serving to room temperature before serving.

Serve yogurt any way it feels comfortable to you and your pet. If a pet is under the weather, it will usually enjoy yogurt as a snack. Feel free to let your pet lick the yogurt right off the spoon, or add a dollop atop their stew. Since everything is best in moderation, a tablespoon is a good serving for any pet.

Cats in particular love the taste and texture of yogurt, so you may find it helpful to incorporate yogurt into your cat's food if you're having difficulty weaning it off its old grain-based, high-carbohydrate food. Yogurt aids in digestion and seems to calm down the "hunger pangs" pets sometimes seem to have in the transition stage. The pangs should last only a few days or a week, but if your cat seems to be ravenously hungry and having a hard time, adding a bit of yogurt may be just what it needs to help ease the transition. This worked like a charm for one always-famished cat, Charlie.

Charlie Cat Licks the Platter Clean

Charlie is a black and white tuxedo cat—very handsome, with a chiseled, pantherlike jaw. Unfortunately, his regal head was not complemented by his pear-shaped body with a huge, white, bowling-ball belly that rested awkwardly low on his hindquarters when he sat up straight. At the young age of eight, it became increasingly difficult for him to reach his back or his tail for grooming, and when he tried to lie sideways, his excess weight seemed to topple him over. Poor Charlie was clearly embarrassed.

As we have all observed, obesity creates limitations for everyone. Before starting our eight-week plan, Charlie had spent three years on all kinds of diets. Most low-calorie and reducing foods left him sad and unsatisfied, which he demonstrated by howling all night long and pushing things off counters, coffee tables, and bookshelves. Charlie was relentless and often took out his frustrations on poor Alex, his svelte and Zen-like Persian sidekick. It's no wonder that Becky, their human companion and a successful marketing director, finally couldn't take the stress and decided to put her paw down. At the end of her own leash, Becky found out about my work with cats and began to pursue the plan with enthusiasm.

Alex took to the stew like the "never do wrong" cat that he was, which seemed to irritate Charlie to no end. Charlie was more reluctant to change and required incentives like tamari, a spoonful of chopped olives, or a beef and herb seasoning. It took a few days, but Charlie soon learned to love his healthy, homemade stew—so much so that it seemed he could never get enough. Even after wolfing down two big bowlfuls, he would continuously beg, complain, and parade through the kitchen pleading for more, and demanding it "Neeooowww!" No amount of treats, cuddling, or kind words could calm him down, and it was a frustrating time for all three.

Charlie's story is not that unusual. For eight years, he was raised on the carbohydrate-filled commercial foods that fill grocery store shelves. Like humans, pets can become addicted to grains, sugar, or other additives, and when they're switched to real food cold turkey, the change may be challenging, as it was for Charlie. For nearly a week, he tried keeping Becky up all night in hopes that she would break down and offer him the junk food he had become addicted to.

Totally unnerved by Charlie's tantrums and practically ready to find him a new home, Becky sought my advice again. She was excited that the solution might be as simple as adding plain, organic yogurt into his food. "Just add a dollop," I told her, "not too much." It took about four days, but it turned out to be the cat's meow. I believe the yogurt provides a coating for the stomach that helps to soothe irritations, both emotional and physical. In addition, the extra fat may make the meal more satisfying. Thankfully it worked, and for the first time in weeks, they all slept peacefully through the night.

During the first month, Charlie steadily dropped weight—nearly three pounds by week three, and six pounds by week eight. The change was so dramatic that Becky's sister didn't even recognize him. His coat is more lustrous than ever (you can see yourself in his black), and his newfound energy is staggering! Now outfitted with a sleek pantherlike body to match his head, Charlie can balance on the back of the sofa again and he's renewed his morning custom of lying in Becky's lap to help with the crossword puzzle.

On the flip side, Alex actually gained a much-needed two pounds on the same diet, which illustrates how important easily digested, real, wholesome, natural food is for our animals. These healthful foods help regulate and maintain proper metabolism, so they can help with problems of either underweight or overweight. Becky makes it a ritual to share a healthy bowl of yogurt with both cats each week, just for the pleasure it brings all of them, and Charlie still loves to lick the platter clean.

Cooking for Cats

Use organic vegetables, organic free-range meats, and/or wild fish whenever possible when cooking for cats. Prepared meals can be stored in individual serving containers in the refrigerator for up to two days for fish dishes and three days for meat; freeze any meals that you need to store for longer. Always serve your cat's food at room temperature. Just before serving, you can add $1/3$ clove garlic, crushed, or 1 teaspoon grated ginger root. I encourage you to add 100 mg (milligrams) of vitamin C powder, too; beyond helping preserve the food (after freezing), it's also one of the most important supplements for your kitty's health. (For more on vitamin C, see chapter 8.)

BIG MACK FOR CATS

Yield: About 10 cups / Serving Size: $1/2$ cup

**$1^1/2$ pounds mackerel fillets or sardines
(fresh, if possible, or frozen, never canned)**

$1/2$ pound green beans, coarsely chopped

$1/2$ pound carrots, coarsely chopped

$1/2$ pound celery, coarsely chopped

1 tablespoon kelp powder

4 to 6 cups springwater

Combine all of the ingredients in a stainless steel pot with enough water to cover. Bring to boil, then lower the heat and simmer for 30 minutes, or until the carrots are tender. Remove from the heat and let cool. With an electric hand mixer, or using a food processor and working in batches, blend all the ingredients into a nice puree. Using ziplock bags or plastic yogurt containers, make up meal-sized portions and freeze whatever you won't use within 2 days.

BIJOUX'S SEAFOOD GUMBO FOR CATS

Yield: About 10 cups / Serving Size: $1/2$ cup

**1$1/2$ pounds wild shrimp (fresh, if possible,
  or frozen, never canned)**

$1/2$ pound celery, coarsely chopped

$1/2$ pound sweet potatoes, coarsely chopped

$1/4$ pound yellow squash, coarsely chopped

$1/4$ pound collard greens, chopped

3 ounces canned clams with juice

2 ounces whole oats

1 tablespoon kelp powder

4 to 6 cups springwater

Combine all of the ingredients in a stainless steel pot with enough water to cover. Bring to a boil, then lower the heat and simmer for 30 minutes, or until the sweet potatoes are tender. Remove from the heat and let cool. With an electric hand mixer, or a food processor and working in batches, blend all the ingredients into a nice puree. Using ziplock bags or plastic yogurt containers, make up meal-sized portions and freeze whatever you won't use within 2 days.

JACK THE CAT'S TURKEY TETRAZZINI

Yield: About 10 cups / Serving Size: $1/2$ cup

1$1/4$ pounds ground turkey

$1/2$ pound yellow squash or pumpkin, coarsely chopped

$1/2$ pound celery, coarsely chopped

$1/4$ pound chicken or turkey liver

1 tablespoon kelp powder

5 to 7 cups springwater

Combine all of the ingredients in a stainless steel pot with enough water to cover. Bring to a boil, then lower the heat and simmer for 30 minutes, or until the vegetables are tender. Remove from the heat and let cool. With an electric hand mixer, or using a food processor and working in batches, blend all the ingredients into a nice puree. Using ziplock bags or plastic yogurt containers, make up meal-sized portions and freeze whatever you won't use within 3 days.

Cooking for Dogs

Use organic vegetables and organic, free-range meats whenever possible. Prepared meals can be stored in individual serving containers in the refrigerator for up to three or four days; freeze any meals that you need to store for longer. Before storing, add a pinch of prevention: ground or powdered rosemary and a crushed clove of garlic will boost your dog's immune system. Serve at room temperature and add 500 mg of vitamin C powder per serving. Not only does it help preserve the food, it's also one of the most important supplements for your dog's health. Garnish with fresh parsley for extra chlorophyll and minerals and better digestion. For all the recipes that follow, use the recommended serving sizes given with the chicken stew recipe on page 90.

BRAVO'S BODACIOUS HEARTY BURGER STEW

Yield: About 9 cups / Serving Size: See page 90

1 pound ground beef or turkey

$^1/_2$ pound millet

$^1/_2$ pound spinach, chopped

$^1/_2$ pound carrots, coarsely chopped

2 cloves garlic, chopped

2 tablespoons kelp powder

4 to 6 cups springwater

Combine all of the ingredients in a stainless steel pot with enough water to cover. Bring to a boil, then lower the heat and simmer for 30 minutes, or until the carrots are tender. Remove from the heat and let cool. With an electric hand mixer, or a food processor and working in batches, blend all the ingredients into a nice puree. Using ziplock bags or plastic yogurt containers, make up meal-sized portions and freeze whatever you won't use in 3 to 4 days.

HEALTHY CORNUCOPIA FOR DOGS

Yield: About 8 cups / Serving Size: See page 90

$1/2$ cup brown rice

$1/2$ cup celery, coarsely chopped

$1/2$ cup carrots, coarsely chopped

$1/2$ cup acorn squash (or yellow squash), coarsely chopped

$1/2$ cup zucchini, coarsely chopped

$1/2$ cup tofu

$1/2$ cup portabella mushrooms, coarsely chopped

1 tablespoon tamari (or natural soy sauce)

Dash of oregano

Dash of rosemary

4 to 6 cups springwater

Combine all the ingredients in a stainless steel pot with enough water to cover. Bring to a boil, then lower the heat, cover, and simmer for 1 hour, or until the rice is tender. Remove from the heat and let cool. Serve at room temperature topped with one or all of the following condiments: Parmesan cheese, yogurt, a sprig of parsley, 1 teaspoon crushed garlic, and 1 teaspoon freshly grated ginger. Using ziplock bags or plastic yogurt containers, make up meal-sized portions and freeze whatever you won't use within 3 or 4 days.

JASMINE'S LAMB DELIGHT

Yield: About 9 cups / Serving Size: See page 90

1 pound ground or chopped lamb meat

$1/2$ pound lamb kidneys, chopped

$1/2$ pound whole barley

$1/2$ pound collard greens, chopped

$1/2$ pound carrots, coarsely chopped

2 tablespoons kelp powder

1 teaspoon dried rosemary

4 to 6 cups springwater

Combine all of the ingredients in a stainless steel pot with enough water to cover. Bring to boil, then lower the heat and simmer for 30 minutes, or until the carrots are soft. Remove from the heat and let cool. With an electric hand mixer, or using a food processor and working in batches, blend all the ingredients into a nice puree. Using ziplock bags or plastic yogurt containers, make up meal-sized portions and freeze whatever you won't use within 3 or 4 days.

SWEETIE'S TURKEY PIE IN A POT

Yield: About 8 cups / Serving Size: See page 90

1 pound ground turkey

$1/_4$ pound organic liver (either turkey or chicken)

$1/_4$ pound whole oats

$1/_4$ pound sweet potatoes, coarsely chopped

$1/_4$ pound celery, coarsely chopped

2 tablespoons kelp powder

2 tablespoons dried oregano

4 to 6 cups springwater

Combine all of the ingredients in a stainless steel pot with enough water to cover. Bring to a boil, then lower the heat and simmer for 30 minutes, or until the barley is soft. Remove from the heat and let cool. With an electric hand mixer, or using a food processor and working in batches, blend all the ingredients into a nice puree. Using ziplock bags or plastic yogurt containers, make up meal-sized portions and freeze whatever you won't use within 3 or 4 days.

Week Two Assessment

❑ Did you throw away all pet-grade foods—canned, kibble, and semimoist? How did it feel?

❑ You prepared an amazing, healthy homemade stew. Was it a chore or a great joy? What can you do to make the process easier?

❑ Are you freezing any portions that can't be used within a few days?

❑ Did your pets gather around the kitchen while the aroma of your creation filled the house with wholesome vitality? Did you tell them it was being made especially for them?

❑ Have you determined a set feeding schedule (twice a day), and are you in tune with how much to feed? Did your pet eat its healthy new stew right away or do you have to use any bribes? Are you comfortable not leaving food down all day? Are you over the guilt?

- ☐ Does your pet seem ravenous for the new food? If so, relax; sometimes it just takes a while for the body to adjust. Don't forget that adding yogurt may help with this.

- ☐ Did you face any challenges in changing your pet's food? Did your pet take right to it or walk away and seem uninterested? Did you put your paw down and stick to the new diet and the schedule? Are you calmly reassuring your pet that this new lifestyle is going to help it feel better? Did you have to add bribe foods, and if so, which ones did you use?

- ☐ What changes in your pet did you notice, physically, emotionally, and in terms of energy? With your continued use of EFAs, you should be starting to notice significant improvements in skin, coat, and energy. Step back, take a deep breath, admire your artistry, and enjoy!

- ☐ Were there any challenges you came up against in actually cooking or preparing the food or feeding twice a day? What were they and how do you think you can resolve them to stay on track with this program? Rest assured that it will become less of a challenge as you get used to the new routine; the more you make the food, the easier it gets to prepare it.

- ☐ What do your friends and family think about your pet's new healthier lifestyle? Are they supportive, or do they think you've gone over the edge? Twenty years ago, people laughed at me for making food for my pets, but now increasing numbers of people are cooking for their pets and recognizing the benefits it provides for the entire household.

- ☐ Do you have any new goals?

Reminder: Logging everything in your journal will show you your true progress week by week.

Daily Play

How did your daily play dates go this week? Did you record them in your Whole Pet Journal? Here are some pet play tips that may prove helpful.

Cat Play Tip: Rotating toys is the best way to keep your kitty stimulated. When you bring out a toy that you've retired for a while, it will seem new and interesting. Or get silly with your cat and have a dance party.

Dog Play Tip: Try wrestling. All dogs engage in this form of play with other dogs, and it can help you and your pup build rapport. I think it's important for you to interact with your dog at the dog level sometimes and allow them to express themselves as dogs do: in rough-and-tumble play. Make sure you don't overexcite any dog too much, and never play rough with an aggressive or fearful dog.

◆ ◆ ◆

In week two, you made a quantum leap in elevating your pet's quality of life. Transforming your pet's main meals is the greatest single catalyst to promoting glorious great health. This fundamental change provides the foundation for everything to come in the rest of the program. Remember, you have the power to provide your dog or cat with more health and vitality than you might have thought possible. Stay close to the ways of nature and you will surely find your way. In week three, you'll remove commercial treats from your pet's diet and substitute fresh, healthy ones. I'll help you learn to use these new treats as both nutrition boosters and rewards.

CHAPTER FIVE

Week Three:
The Art of the Treat

In your journal:

- Complete the Weekly Checkup.

- Schedule your daily play dates.

- Throughout the week, fill in the Week at a Glance.

- At week's end, complete the Weekly Assessment.

This week you'll add some smart snacking to your pet's new diet. At this point, you're feeding your pet a natural diet supplemented with essential fatty acids, and by tossing the store-bought foods, you've removed a significant amount of antagonistic elements from its body. The next step is to eliminate the last of the low-quality grains, sugars, salts, and ingredients hiding in your pet's snacks. Now is the time to sneak in a veggie or add extra garlic, more healthy protein, additional greens, fresh berries, or whatever your particular pet needs more of in its diet to feel happy and get healthier. As an added bonus, wholesome treats can be used as bribes for almost any purpose, including behavior training and easing the transition to the new diet.

We all love snacks; the exciting indulgence associated with an extra tidbit can be totally gratifying. Treats energize us, as well as reward and inspire us, and, like forbidden fruit, make us feel a little wanton, wild, and untamed. From your pet's viewpoint, treats represent love and adoration from you. Giving your pet spontaneous snacks is fine, as long as they're given in moderation and chosen wisely. In your quest to elevate your pet's health, you must reach for healthful choices in everything you offer. Using nutritionally dense treats accomplishes these goals and enhances the process.

It's important to define *treat* as something the pet does not get on a regular basis. You're going to use treats as beneficial snacks or rewards—an incentive for your pet doing something well, even if it's just being a pet. It's up to you to set some limits, because pets are exceedingly good at being pets—and too much of a good thing can be problematic.

Treats are effective training aids, but I also like to offer them with a specific health purpose or ailment in mind, as a *treat*-ment, so to speak: to enhance the digestive system, to fortify a feeling of well-being, or to ease the transition to a new food or diet. In my view, treats are more than just a reward and a gastronomic indulgence; they're integral to a daily nourishment rhythm. Treats help keep your pet's blood sugar level from spiking, regulate its metabolism to burn fat more efficiently, and round out a nutritionally balanced diet. So snacks deserve the same careful planning and preparation as your pet's main meals.

What to Expect

Very excited dogs and cats. New tricks. Big purrs. Lips smacking. Tail wagging. Face licking, dancing, prancing, and lots of begging for more. Not to mention a few back flips here and there. By following my smart snack plan, you can keep your pet's hunger pangs at bay while enhancing its health.

Project: Make Way for Healthy Treats

This week's project is a two-parter. First, it is time to 'fess up and come clean. I want you to toss out all commercial treats, including chemically laced or artificially flavored rawhide chews (see sidebar). To truly change your pet's diet and get in the spirit of this eight-week plan, it's not enough to get rid of commercial foods; all the biscuits, cookies, crunchies, and grain-laden snacks must go, as well. If you haven't done so already, throw out all the commercial pet treats, including the ones in the laundry room and other hiding places. No cheating! I promise you won't be without delicious treats this week.

For the second part of the project, throw a treat-tasting party for your pet. Make up four or five of the easy snack recipes in this chapter (pages 127–129). Then arrange them on a party tray or line them up in a row and let your pet choose the ones it likes best. If you end up with any leftovers (not likely unless you're making them up in bulk), you can store them in snack-size ziplock baggies. As your pet's taste for healthier foods develops, you'll be able to serve up a wider variety of nutritious snacks and season them with tasty condiments that excite its senses and appeal to its individual palate. Have fun and "bone" appétit!

Treats as Between-Meal Snacks

As discussed in chapter 2, cats and dogs naturally rotate through cycles of feast and famine. Giving your pet a small snack or treat during its fasting phase (between meals) will help you feel it isn't starving. It also builds a stronger relationship between you, as caregiver, and your animal. Start your pet's day with a healthy breakfast. If you're around to do it, offer a midmorning light treat or a midday mini meal for a larger pet. Serve your pet a hearty dinner and feel free to give it a light treat later in the evening. If you're not at home during the day, hide a treat in different places for your pet to find. This will get them up and hunting!

Watch Out for "Natural" Treats

You may have some treats on hand that claim to be "all natural." There's one variety I find especially problematic: the jerky-style treat for dogs. Pet food manufacturers are marketing more products that resemble snacks made for humans these days. The idea seems to be that pet owners want to treat their animals to a version of the treats that people enjoy. Jerky treats are especially disturbing because they can be labeled "all natural," and as a result, many caring pet owners are rather unsuspecting of what they actually contain, how they're made, or why they're not good for dogs. In order to dry any kind of meat and label it "jerky," it must be processed with huge amounts of salt in order to preserve it. Salt is a natural ingredient, but when overused it can have harmful effects on the heart and kidneys, and this is even more true for animals than for humans. Observe your pet closely; if it runs to the water bowl after a treat, it's likely that the treat contains too much salt. Make conscious, careful decisions in everything you choose for your pet and pay careful attention to how it reacts.

Chew bones or biscuits with colors can be equally bad, even the ones that claim to be healthy or natural. Most people don't make a connection that a mere chew toy or treat could harm their pet, but we have to condition ourselves to look at the whole picture and learn to make certain assessments. These seemingly innocuous products are too often overlooked as a potential cause of health problems. I have seen some of the toughest chronic skin and digestive problems clear up in a few days when some of these chews were eliminated.

In 1999, the FDA issued a nationwide public health advisory about contaminated pet chews derived from beef or pork in the form of pigs' ears, beef jerky treats, smoked hooves, pigs' skins, and the like. They warned that people who come into contact with these chews might be at risk of bacterial infections causing flulike symptoms. Though they didn't address pet safety, if these products aren't safe for you to handle, how can it be healthy for your pet to chew on them? Improvements have since been made to these products, but I'm still skeptical about their ingredients and their safety. In fact, a popular rawhide chew made from USDA-certified beef hides, allegedly free of bacteria and preservatives, has a label that reads both "natural" and "not for human consumption." Again, if it's not safe for you, chances are it's not beneficial for your pet's health. Remember that pet-grade standards and all that they imply are applicable to everything you buy for your pet.

Here's a final warning about rawhide: if it's slimy, goopy, sticky, and falling apart after it's been chewed on, it was probably treated with formaldehyde and arsenic as preservatives, which are now leaching out. Even so-called natural rawhide may be coated with flavor additives. Although salt and arsenic actually are natural substances, neither is beneficial to your animal's health.

Treats and Diabetes or Obesity

Regulated meals and snacking are particularly important for diabetic and overweight pets, and a diet consisting of meat and vegetables has been shown to be highly effective for both of these conditions. By feeding these types of food to your pet at regular mealtimes and for between-meal snacks, you can keep your pet's blood sugar stabilized throughout the day. You'll help the body regulate its metabolism and natural insulin production more efficiently. Insulin, a hormone secreted by the pancreas, transports sugar from the blood into the cells. When the pancreas malfunctions because of a high-carbohydrate diet or too many sugary foods, glucose can accumulate in the blood, creating elevated blood sugar levels.

These interconnected factors of lowering carbohydrate intake, eliminating processed sugars, and reducing weight are essential to achieving great health. Insulin injections can be used to lower blood sugar levels, but without a change in diet, this only masks symptoms and holds the disease at bay. Diabetes and obesity have become shockingly common afflictions among pets, but fortunately most holistic veterinarians now understand the connection between these conditions and the high quantities of grain (particularly corn) in so many pet foods. Hopefully, this understanding of the importance of high-quality food and regular feeding schedules will soon become mainstream.

Obesity is linked to many health problems beyond diabetes, including joint and back problems, skin conditions, and liver, heart, or kidney disease. So even if diabetes isn't an issue, a conscientious pet owner will recognize the importance of providing treats composed of real foods that support the body in functioning efficiently at any age. Treats should add to your pet's good health, not detract from it—as the story of a dog named Shadow illustrates.

Gloria and Shadow: "Just One More Cookie"

Shadow was a nine-year-old black terrier mix. Unfortunately, Shadow was wider than she was long—an odd and troubling configuration for a dog. Her weight problem had been taking quite a toll on her health. She had difficulty walking, her breathing was labored, and she had recently developed irritable bowel syndrome (IBS), straining for long periods of time trying to eliminate.

Gloria didn't realize how much damage she was doing by feeding Shadow those clean-looking grain-filled biscuits, which she purchased in the large, economy-size box. "What can I do? She always seems so hungry, and I'm afraid she won't love me if I stop giving her treats." Gloria couldn't seem to resist Shadow's big, brown eyes, and Shadow certainly had a way of wrapping Gloria around her finger.

As Shadow's condition worsened, Gloria desperately consulted everyone she knew for ideas. When she heard about the good results I'd had with so many sick pets, she contacted me. With Shadow on her last legs, Gloria started feeding her homemade chicken stew just in the nick of time. She didn't mind cooking for her "little" girl, but she was totally shocked at the way Shadow wolfed her food down in the first few weeks. "She's going to eat me right out of house and home." I calmed her down by explaining that many pets, especially the ones who are overweight, actually have organs that have become depleted from lack of proper nutrition, but their bodies will finally become sated when presented with real, easily digested food. Gloria was relieved to hear that her dog's ravenous appetite would settle down as soon as Shadow's organs soaked up all of the great nutrition her body was so desperate to take in.

In about two weeks' time, Shadow's body found its proper metabolism and she began eating normally, and within six weeks she gracefully lost all the unwanted pounds. At the end of the seventh week, Gloria called me to let me know that Shadow was doing amazingly well, her coat became lustrous, and it no longer matted and was easier to care for because of the great nutrition. Her improved health was dramatically displayed by her sleek new figure and the energy that seemed to appear out of nowhere. The only disappointment was that Shadow still had trouble relieving herself. "Some days she's constipated, and other days it's like mush!"

Knowing full well that this was contrary to how my plan works, I had to pry the rest of the story out of Gloria, further honing my expert interrogation skills. After a long list of grueling questions, I finally uncovered the cause: Gloria was still feeding Shadow dog biscuits because of her guilt about changing Shadow's diet so dramatically. Old habits die hard. "She loves those biscuits, you know. I couldn't stop myself. It's only two or three cookies a day. What else can I give her for treats?" Well, as long as you're asking: celery, apples, carrot sticks, chicken, sardines, cottage cheese. . . . To this day, Gloria is still amazed that Shadow loves her healthy, digestible carrot sticks as much as she did the biscuits, if not more, and ever since Gloria tossed out that last biscuit, bowel trouble is a thing of Shadow's past.

Treat Basics

I group the foods that lend themselves to healthy, tasty treats into four categories: dairy and fruit, eggs, meat, and vegetables. The following sections present background information, serving ideas, and recipes for each category. But first, there are a couple of basic guidelines that apply to all treats:

- All treats can be made ahead of time and refrigerated or frozen, but always bring them to room temperature before serving.

- Adjust portion sizes to your pet's size, just as you do with main meals. For cats, make treats about the size of the end joint of your finger or thumb (about an inch). Give small dogs a thumb-size treat; larger dogs can have two thumbs worth.

DAIRY AND FRUIT

I group dairy and fruit into one category, as they tend to blend together well. Organic yogurt (discussed in the previous chapter) and cottage cheese (in moderation) are healthy and delicious snacks, and I've never heard of any pet who didn't love the taste of both. I emphasize moderation because most pasteurized dairy products can cause mucus to form. Cottage cheese, however, is healthful, does not clog pets up, and is fairly easy to digest. Here's a great idea: take a small scoop of either dairy product and add it to a platter of dark leafy greens; top with grated carrot or a teaspoon of berries for an added antioxidant advantage.

When creating treats, consider both your animal's tastes and its health concerns. With their ample phytonutrients, fruits are often useful foods for healing. For example, if your pet suffers from urinary tract infections, bladder stones, or other urinary tract problems, try adding a small amount of natural blueberry powder to help acidify the urine. Since blueberries in their natural state are quite sweet, most pets enjoy them in any form. However, never opt for anything with added sugar. Animal studies are now proving that blueberries are also good for the heart. Rich in antioxidants, blueberries have excellent antiaging properties; they help improve vision and increase brainpower, and also support the nervous system, balance, and coordination. Melon is another great fruit snack. My cat Spot's favorite treat of all time was a ripe, juicy cantaloupe ball. Pets usually love the flavor, and cantaloupe is an excellent diuretic. (The healing powers of vitamin C and other antioxidants, and the foods rich in them, will be covered in detail in chapter 8.)

Caution: When it comes to fresh fruit, a little goes a long way for pets. Too much fruit can cause fermentation in the digestive tract and create an upset stomach or diarrhea, so use these treats sparingly. An inch of papaya for a small pet or two inches for a larger one can be added to a meal to aid in digestion. A couple of blueberries in a shake or as a snack topping will add important antioxidants. A juicy cantaloupe ball or two is perfect once a week.

EGGS

Eggs are a high-energy, high-quality source of protein, making them great snacks for pets, but it's important that you use free-range, organic eggs. Offer egg treats occasionally, perhaps once or twice weekly. Hard-boiled eggs can be chopped and sprinkled over their food as a bribe or sliced and served as a little hors d'oeuvres. You can also try scrambling them lightly or sharing a bit of your Sunday morning omelet. An omelet filled with a variety of vegetables is a great way to get your whole family eating all their needed greens with gusto!

Many well-respected holistic vets recommend mixing raw eggs into pets' food because raw eggs would be a natural part of most predators' diet in the wild. On the other hand, some people feel the egg white should be cooked but that raw yoke is fine. Above all, eggs must be fresh to reduce any chances of contamination by harmful bacteria. While most holistic vets feel that salmonella poisoning probably isn't a problem for domesticated dogs and cats, you need to decide for yourself.

All my pets get whole, raw, organic egg as a small meal once or twice a week. I beat the egg slightly with a fork so that it's blended, making it easier for them to eat or slurp up. Both of my cats love it this way. Many a pet who's under the weather or refuses to eat will perk up and enjoy a cool, freshly beaten egg, served by itself or with a dollop of organic yogurt mixed in. I feel their bodies know instinctively what's good for them.

Caution: Before serving a raw egg, you can test it for freshness. Be sure the yolk is whole and the white is somewhat congealed (not runny like water). Smell it for freshness and poke the yoke gently with your pinkie; it should be firm. The yoke should be bright yellow to dark orange; the darker and closer to orange in color, the more nutritious. In fact, hens fed kelp often lay eggs that have a reddish orange yolk.

MEAT

High-quality meat-based snacks are excellent for several reasons:

- All pets, both cats and dogs, enjoy eating meat.

- Meat-based snacks are nutritious and provide easily assimilated protein, fat, and vitamins.

- They're easy to shop for and prepare.

- They assist finicky eaters in the transition from pet-grade products.

- They're low in calories and carbohydrate and won't cause weight gain.

VEGETABLES

If you're feeding your pet healthy, homemade stews from recipes in this book, you've already seen the benefits of vegetables in your pet's diet. Smart vegetable snacks will provide even more. They're so healthful that I never worry about overusing them, although I do recommend against feeding cruciferous vegetables (broccoli, Brussels sprouts, cabbage, and cauliflower) to animals due to their gas-generating properties. If your pet enjoys vegetables, offer it a wide variety. You want to supply as many of Mother Nature's colors as possible to provide the broadest palette of nutrients.

Dogs and cats love pumpkin as a snack, and it's easy to add this excellent vegetable to your pet's daily regime using canned pumpkin (100 percent pumpkin with no added spices) and pumpkin seeds. As mentioned in chapter 4, pumpkin has a great nutritional profile. In fact, the Chinese consider it a symbol of health and prosperity and refer to it as the "emperor of the garden." Low in calories and high in vitamin A and fiber, it's often used to treat both diarrhea and constipation in pets. It lubricates the digestive system and provides soft bulk, so it can help long-haired cats pass hairballs through their system. Pumpkin seeds, which benefit the urinary tract and help eliminate parasites, are also useful. As far as healing properties are concerned, pumpkin is a top ten holistic healing food. Gregory Todd, DVM, a holistic veterinarian who specializes in Chinese medicine for pets, first introduced me to the importance of this versatile vegetable, and he's kindly provided more information on pumpkin in the accompanying sidebar.

Treat Recipes

Try making a party platter with three or four of the goodies in this section (sounds like part two of this week's project, doesn't it?). Then treat your pets (and yourself!) to some smart snacking. Any of the following quick snacks can also be used in larger or smaller amounts as bribes; use them as toppings on healthy meals to help win your pet over to the new food. Just as with main meals, treats should be served at or near room temperature. Try brushing any of the treats you make yourself with your EFA oil blend. This way your pet will associate the oil's aroma and taste with the treats they love.

READY-TO-EAT TREATS FOR DOGS AND CATS

- Cantaloupe balls
- A whole, raw organic egg beaten together well with yogurt or cottage cheese
- Organic baby food
- Yogurt mixed with a few raspberries or blueberries
- Sardines (fresh or frozen)
- Organic cheese on a salt-free cracker

READY-TO-EAT TREATS FOR DOGS

- Celery sticks (plain or with unsalted peanut butter or cottage cheese)
- Carrot sticks (plain or with yogurt)
- Apple slices (with or without peanut butter)
- Green beans

EASY-TO-MAKE TREATS FOR DOGS OR CATS

Voyko loves to pamper pets just as much as I do, as you can see from this treat he makes for our whole family of critters. Buy a few pounds of raw chicken or turkey liver. Organic is especially important here; because the liver is an organ of detoxification, it contains higher levels of toxins than other body tissues. You can substitute any other type of meat if you're not comfortable with liver.

VOYKO'S PAW-LICKIN' LIVER TREATS

Yield: 40 servings / Serving Size: 1 ounce

3 pounds chicken or turkey liver

Fresh or dried oregano (optional)

Fresh or dried rosemary (optional)

Minced fresh garlic (optional)

Preheat the oven to 325°F. Place the liver on a large baking pan and sprinkle the herbs on top. Bake for about 30 minutes. Remove from the oven and let cool, then dice the liver into 1-inch cubes. Put a few ounces into individual ziplock bags, and freeze the portions that won't be eaten right away. Your healthy, homemade treats will stay fresh in the refrigerator for 2 to 3 days, and up to a month in the freezer.

SHRIMP AND EGGS

Yield: 1 serving / Serving Size: $1/2$ cup

1 teaspoon butter

1 medium-sized wild shrimp, diced

1 egg, beaten

$1/4$ teaspoon garlic powder

1 teaspoon grated Parmesan cheese

1 teaspoon plain yogurt

Melt the butter in a small skillet over medium heat. Add the shrimp and sauté for a moment, then add the egg and cook until just set. Stir in the garlic powder and turn off the heat. Cool to room temperature, then top with Parmesan cheese and yogurt, before serving.

SALMON AND VEGGIE PATTIES

Yield: 4 servings / Serving Size: 1 $1/_2$-inch patty

$1/_4$ cup coarsely chopped green beans

$1/_4$ cup coarsely chopped sweet
  potatoes

$1/_4$ cup coarsely chopped zucchini

$1/_4$ cup coarsely chopped yellow squash

$1/_2$ cup springwater

$1/_2$ pound wild salmon

$1/_4$ cup orange juice

1 teaspoon grated Parmesan cheese

1 teaspoon plain yogurt

Combine the green beans, sweet potatoes, zucchini, yellow squash, and water in a large skillet over medium heat. Bring to a boil, then add the salmon. Cover and steam for 5 minutes, or until the fish flakes easily when tested with a fork. Cool to room temperature, then transfer to a food processor. Add the orange juice, Parmesan cheese, and yogurt and blend well. Shape into patties and either serve right away or store in the refrigerator. Freeze any portions you won't use within 2 to 3 days.

LUNCHTIME SALAD TREAT

Yield: 2 servings / Serving Size: $1/_2$ cup

$1/_2$ cup chopped wild shrimp, deboned organic chicken,
  or wild crabmeat, cooked and cooled

$1/_2$ cup mixed salad greens

1 tablespoon chopped alfalfa or red clover sprouts

1 teaspoon olive oil

1 tablespoon cottage cheese or plain yogurt

In a small bowl, toss and combine the shrimp, salad greens, sprouts, and olive oil. Transfer to serving dishes and top with the cottage cheese before serving. Freeze any portions you won't use within 2 to 3 days.

LIVER PÂTÉ

Yield: 4 to 6 servings / Serving Size: 2 tablespoons

1 tablespoon butter

$^1/_2$ pound fresh liver (beef, chicken, turkey, or duck)

$^1/_2$ teaspoon garlic powder

1 teaspoon dried rosemary

1 hard-boiled egg

1 teaspoon chopped fresh parsley

Melt the butter in a skillet over medium heat. Sauté the liver, turning frequently until lightly browned on all sides. Stir in the garlic powder and rosemary, then turn off the heat and cool to room temperature. Transfer to food processor, add the hard-boiled egg and chopped parsley, and process until smooth. Store in the refrigerator for 2 to 3 days, and freeze any portions you won't use within that time period.

STEAK TARTARE

Yield: Approximately 24 balls
Serving Size: 2 to 3 balls for a cat or small dog; 4 to 6 balls for a medium or larger dog

$^1/_4$ cup crushed bulgur wheat

1 cup springwater

$^1/_2$ pound ground chicken, beef, or turkey

1 egg

1 teaspoon chopped garlic

2 tablespoons chopped fresh parsley

1 tablespoon olive oil

1 tablespoon tamari or soy sauce

2 tablespoon chopped fresh spinach

Soak the bulgur in the springwater overnight. The next day, drain any remaining water from the bulgur, then mix in all the remaining ingredients. Roll into 1-inch balls and serve. These raw treats must be eaten within 24 hours.

Treat Time–Savers

If you don't have time to make your own treats, don't despair. I have some time-saving tips for you. Treat making can be something you do while cooking for yourself and your family. Whenever you cook turkey, lamb, liver, beef, shrimp, or fish for yourself, cook a little extra for your pet. Cut your pet's portion into one-inch pieces, place them in a ziplock bag, and store them in the refrigerator for two or three days, freezing whatever you can't use in that time frame. These handy bites can be given as is, used in a shake, or added to a heartier mini meal.

Also, keep an eye out for the higher-quality treats on the market these days. Your local health food store probably sells freeze-dried pet treats made with only all-natural USDA-approved meats fit for human consumption. What's great about these snacks is they're simply pure protein, which is ideal for any cat or dog at any age. They contain no added sugar, salt, fillers, grains, or chemicals. You don't risk throwing off any essential balance in the body when you offer your pet these tasty morsels.

Alicia and Simba: Bribery Will Get You Everywhere!

Alicia couldn't wait to get home from work on Monday. She was sure that this would be the momentous day she would actually get to touch the elusive feral kitten who was living in the crawl space under her house. She had been feeding the little orange waif for several weeks but could never get close enough to the skittish kitten that spooked whenever anything moved. It broke her heart to think that she might never get to hold this pretty kitty.

But over the weekend, Alicia had tuned in to a radio interview in which I described in detail how simple it was to make Voyko's healthy liver treats, and how no cat could resist them. So Monday, on her way home from work, she stopped off at the butcher shop to pick up some fresh organic turkey liver. As soon as she got home, she baked the liver with finely chopped garlic to bring out the great flavor. You could almost taste the aroma as it drifted out her open front door.

As Alicia sat cross-legged on the front porch and focused on positive thoughts, her dream came true. The lovely little cat came right to her and proceeded to take the delectable treats right out of her hand! Overcome with shock and excitement, Alicia was breathless. It was the beginning of a beautiful love affair, and the trust between the two of them grew stronger over the next few days. With tears in her voice, Alicia called to let me know how happy she was and that this wild cat had finally settled down. It's easy to calm the savage beast with the right food!

Hold the Spices

Lady and the Tramp may have been onto something when they shared that plateful of spaghetti and meatballs. Micki Voisard, a master dog chef featured on the DVD *Eat, Drink, and Wag Your Tail*, claims to have cured herself and her three dogs from cancer with a food-based approach. She recommends Italian food, with its fresh vegetables, herbs, olive oil, cheeses, and pasta, as a nutritious meal, or mini meal for dogs.

The sauce and meatballs are fine on rare occasions, though we recommend keeping the pasta portion to a minimum (and none at all for cats). But remember the old Alka-Seltzer commercial, "Mama mia, that's a spicy meatball"? You may enjoy spicy foods, but please omit the spices when cooking for your pet, as they can cause gas, irritate the stomach lining, and upset the digestive system. I've found that dogs and cats do much better when they eat simply prepared, plain meals, so make sure your homemade meals border on bland. Your pet will stay healthier in the long run.

Week Three Assessment

- ❏ Are all forms of commercial, chemical-laden, grain-based foods and treats gone from your household? Are you sure? Nothing hiding on top of the refrigerator?

- ❏ What yummy treats did you make for your pet? When and how did you use them? Be specific: for rewards, training, bribes?

- ❏ What are your pet's favorite snacks? Are you using any bribes at all and for what purpose? Have you tasted any of your pet's treats? Are you comparing how you treat yourself to snacks and how you want to treat your pet? Do you see any correlation? Are you tuned in to eating healthier foods yourself at this point?

- ❏ Are you keeping your treats to a small amount daily?

- ❏ When you change your own habits, your pet's will change as well. Did you notice any of your old unhealthy habits fading away?

Daily Play

Ten minutes a day should now be trivial. Add another five minutes or go for two ten-minute sessions.

Cat Play Tip: Take a small sock and fill it with fresh catnip and a sheet of tissue paper. The tissue paper will make a crinkling sound that will double-delight your cat's senses for days. Tie up the open end of the sock to keep all the contents inside. Your cat will love this kind of toy because it can get its teeth into the sock and hold it easily with its claws. Toss the sock across the floor and watch your cat scurry along to catch it. This toy will keep your cat occupied until it's time for a lovely catnap.

Catnip Caution: There's nothing wrong with a little "nip" now and then. Most people understand that an occasional cocktail is just fine, and the same holds true for catnip. But too much of a good thing is no good, and catnip is no exception. Use it sparingly: once or twice weekly, but not more than that. You don't want your cat to become bored with it or immune to its delicious aroma, so a little nip every few days is more than enough. My own cats love to sniff, eat, and roll all over this herb. And one thing's for certain, organic catnip is always the best!

Dog Play Tip: Tug-of-war is one of my dogs' favorite games, and it's probably your dog's favorite game, too. I use a pure cotton rope toy with some strength to it because my dogs can pull hard. When your dog has one end in its mouth, pull gently to build some resistance. Don't pull so hard that you might hurt your dog, just firmly enough for it to be both safe and fun. This form of play is great exercise for both of you; you're both guaranteed to build muscles. You owners of larger dogs know what I mean!

◆ ◆ ◆

You've cleared away all unhealthful treats or chews and replaced them with your own fresh snacks and rewards. It's been an eye-opening week, as your pet's snacking choices have likely expanded from the few commercial choices—grain-laden biscuits and crunchies, fake "people meats," and potentially dangerous chews and jerky—to an almost limitless range of fresh, whole, healthy treats. In the coming week, you'll add the healing and energizing power of green foods to your pet's diet, and you'll free your yard and home of any pesticides and poisonous plants that could endanger your pet.

CHAPTER SIX

Week Four:
The Art of the Sun

In your journal:

- Complete the Weekly Checkup.

- Schedule your daily play dates.

- Throughout the week, fill in the Week at a Glance.

- At week's end, complete the Weekly Assessment.

Color it brightly! This week, get ready to get even healthier as we paint the food bowl green with cereal grasses, which include alfalfa, wheatgrass, barley grass, and algae (such as spirulina and chlorella). Known as "green foods," these are a must for the well-fed pet. These nutrient-dense foods are a step above typical leafy green vegetables because they possess immense sources of beta-carotene, protein, and chlorophyll, the photosynthetic pigment in plants. In fact, a mere teaspoon of cereal grass contains far more chlorophyll than a handful of green vegetables. So a day without greens really is like a day without sunshine. Read on and learn about the importance of green foods and how to infuse your pet with a sun-kissed energy source so potent that it can help keep your furry friend strong and free of disease.

What to Expect

More vitality and boundless energy, and no more nibbling on potted plants or grass. Greens make any couch potato want to get up and dance, so pay particular attention during play dates. As your pet's energy levels soar to new heights, you'll want to have your video camera handy.

I take slight offense (admittedly, it's very slight) to the old cliché about watching the grass grow. If you really knew the importance of what's going on inside a single blade of grass and how beneficial it can be to your pets, you might very well start a sod farm. Pets don't eat grass just to vomit; the truth is that most native peoples and nearly all animals eat green plants or grass daily if they have access to it. Yes, it's cleansing, and animals, particularly cats, often purge in times of illness. However, the reasons animals eat grass mainly involve enzymes, digestion, and disease prevention, and your pet most definitely eats grass and plants because it needs chlorophyllins—the sun's energy in a form fit for a pet's body.

As you read this chapter, I'd like you to think of all the green foods as healing herbs filled with therapeutic properties. I'll show you how to choose, cultivate, and use the most outstanding green foods to maximize their anti-inflammatory properties. The secret of greens, according to both Eastern and Western medicines, is their ability to successfully activate and renew the body at the cellular level while helping keep all those nasty free radicals at bay. Free radicals, a product of oxidation, cause the body to age prematurely. But if you can fight them off, you can assure your pet a longer life filled with greater vitality. Green foods are also recognized for having positive effects on the immune system, cholesterol, and blood pressure, and they have anticancer properties as well.

Project: A Chemical-Free Zone

If your pet spends time outdoors, your project this week is to take an inventory of everything used on your lawn or in your garden—fertilizers, pesticides, herbicides, and so on. You need to be aware of what those chemicals might be doing to your pet, whether through ingestion or just contact. It's fairly obvious that anything a pet walks on is likely to get into its body; we've all seen animals lick their paws. If you live in a condo or apartment, talk with the lawn maintenance crew and the exterminators to find out what they apply to the areas where your pet walks. If you have indoor plants, find out if any are toxic if ingested, and if so, give them to someone who doesn't have pets. Also take a good look at what's in your plant food or fertilizer. I've included a brief list of common potentially harmful plants below, but if you grow a lot of plants, please do some research to determine if you have others that may be problematic. You can find many lists of plants toxic to animals on the Internet.

Plants to Avoid Inside or Out

Before we delve into beneficial greens and the plants that produce them, I want to point out some potentially dangerous plants. Many of those listed below are fatal if eaten, and in some cases certain plant parts, such as flowers, are safe, whereas other parts, such as stems or seedpods, are poisonous. Many poisonous plants are so common and seemingly innocuous that you'd never suspect that they're toxic. The beautiful oleander bush is a prime example. It's grown all over the country and is particularly prolific here in Florida. I knew it was poisonous, but I was surprised to learn it contains a deadly heart stimulant similar to the drug digitalis! I was even more shocked to hear that people have actually died from eating foods speared on oleander branches and roasted over a fire. Check with your state's health department for a list of poisonous plants in your neck of the woods; these lists are often available online.

Toxic Plants

- Autumn crocus
- Azalea
- Bleeding heart
- Bulbs such as hyacinth, narcissus, and daffodil
- Cactus
- Chile peppers

- Dieffenbachia (dumb cane)
- Elephant ear
- Foxglove
- Iris
- Jasmine
- Larkspur
- Laurel

- Lily of the valley
- Monkshood
- Oleander
- Rhododendron
- Star of Bethlehem
- Wisteria
- Yew

The Miracle of Chlorophyll

Photosynthesis was, I believe, the first five-syllable word I learned or cared to know. The process fascinated me for many reasons. Beyond the thrill of seeing seeds sprout, grow, and bloom before my eyes, I loved to imagine how my plants captured sunlight and, like an electric power plant, converted it to chemical energy. Every single day brings visible changes, unfolding, and blossoming, and the same holds true for pets eating their greens. Chlorophyll is instrumental in this process. It is the substance that makes plants green, and it helps capture the energy in the form of light necessary for photosynthesis. It plays an important role in transporting oxygen throughout the plant as well, because the energy absorbed by chlorophyll transforms carbon dioxide and water into carbohydrates and oxygen. In fact, antiaging expert Nicholas Perricone, MD, likens chlorophyll in plants to the hemoglobin in animals' blood—essential to life. So, from here on, if I mention green foods, automatically include chlorophyll in your thoughts, because it provides the natural energy that is the essence of green foods.

Green foods enhance life and healing at the cellular level. They perform miracles of all kinds: many have anti-inflammatory and antioxidant properties or stimulate the renewal of RNA and DNA, making them useful in the treatment of degenerative diseases and in the reversal of aging. This last property is the focus of many recent studies on green foods, as they may well be the fountain of youth.

When it comes to longevity, we would do well to emulate the Japanese. Although they live in densely populated, high-pressure urban areas like many of the pet owners most in need of this book, they exhibit remarkable health and longevity. This may be due, in part, to their diet, which is rich in sea vegetables and algae. A remarkable survival story developed in Japan after World War II, when people in the areas around Hiroshima and Nagasaki developed cancer at much lower rates than expected. The Japanese attribute this to immune system support from chlorella, a miraculous green algae. In *Prescription for Dietary Wellness*, Phyllis A. Balch explains that "Chlorella . . . contains the highest chlorophyll level per ounce of any plant, as well as protein (nearly 58 percent), carbohydrates, all of the B vitamins, vitamins C and E, amino acids (including all eight of the essential ones), enzymes and rare trace minerals." It's no wonder that green foods are commonly called "super foods."

Everyone benefits from eating green foods, but they're especially important for city pets and apartment dwellers. Most cats kept in an urban environment never set foot outdoors, so it's important to provide them with greens throughout their lives. Although most city dogs are walked outside, they don't have access to the variety of healthful live foods that their country counterparts do. Preparing living green foods for your pet, no matter where you live, gives it the great green life nature intended. Fresh chlorophyllins provide antioxidants, aid digestion, and keep your pet from eating your potted plants and grass. Give your pet a garden of its own and watch your furry friend blossom with glowing great health!

Green food supplements proved to be a lifesaver for one cat owner when she and her pet had to adjust to a new life in the big city.

Mika: Always a Country Girl

Terry was aghast at the prospect of moving from her sprawling home on five lush, tree-lined acres in North Carolina to a two-bedroom apartment in Manhattan's Greenwich Village. She had difficulty imagining adjusting to the new surroundings. Her husband, Jeff, who had been transferred by his company, assured her that both she and their tabby cat, Mika, would adapt easily, but Terry's garden meant everything to her. It had become an important part of her meditation, and she looked forward to the weekends, when she and Mika lingered together for hours out on the sprawling lawns taking in the country air and enjoying the perennials she worked so lovingly to maintain.

Jeff assured her the large, screened balcony in the new apartment would provide her with enough room to keep a small garden and that Mika would adjust to the modified living conditions. When they moved in, Terry tried to make the best of things and began to create her own little haven in the city by designing a small but impressive array of potted plants, ficus trees, and herbs. All was going well until Terry arrived home one day to find that several of her plants had been mangled and destroyed. At first she thought parasites might be the problem, but then she realized that Mika was responsible. She scolded Mika and ran through the house chasing the petrified cat, who didn't know what she had done or where to hide next.

Terry, always a proactive kind of gal, knew she had to solve the dilemma somehow, and she wasn't willing to give up her garden or the cat. She figured that Mika must be missing something in nature that she wasn't getting in her new city lifestyle. Terry asked everyone she could think of about it, and eventually her tenacity and resourcefulness paid off. An employee at her local health food store recommended she give Mika a super green supplement that included a variety of herbs, plants, and berries and was perfectly suited to a city cat's needs. Terry never came home to another episode of horror garden, and Mika benefited from the supplement for the rest of her life. But the true happy ending came about a year later, when the entire family was able to move out into the country again, where they could all breathe a little easier.

The Green Foods

The term *green foods* embraces a collection of nutrient-rich plants: algae, such as spirulina and chlorella; cereal grasses like wheatgrass and barley grass; and all manner of sprouts, alfalfa being the most familiar. (Alfalfa is Voyko's favorite plant food for pets; check out his Liver and Greens Shake recipe on the facing page). Let's look at each of these green foods in a bit more detail. In the sections below, I'll also give you some recipes and tips for incorporating these nutritional powerhouses into your pet's diet.

ALFALFA

Literally translated, *alfalfa* means "the father of all foods." Arabs discovered alfalfa and gave it this name because it made their horses swift and strong. Not surprisingly, alfalfa is the hay of choice among horse owners. Alfalfa reportedly contains all the vitamins, minerals, and trace elements known to be needed for human and animal health. It's safe for kittens and puppies, and it may help nursing mothers produce more milk.

The Chinese, who have long valued alfalfa's medicinal powers, have used it for centuries to treat fluid retention, swelling, and kidney stones. It's great for the urinary tract and the intestines, as it has remarkable detoxifying properties. Alfalfa is most often consumed by humans in sprout form, but it's also available as a dried herb or powder. Because of concerns about food-borne illness, commercially grown alfalfa sprouts are usually prepackaged and rinsed in chlorine, so it's much better to grow them yourself. If your thumb isn't particularly green, or if planting and harvesting isn't your thing, buy some organic alfalfa powder or dried alfalfa to add to your pet's meals. But for Voyko's Liver and Greens Shake you really need fresh alfalfa sprouts. Every cat and dog I know loves this shake. Although it's packed with greens, the liver gives it a deep purple hue.

VOYKO'S LIVER AND GREENS SHAKE

Yield: 4 servings / Serving Size: $^1/_2$ cup

1 tablespoon butter

$^1/_2$ pound fresh liver (beef, chicken, turkey, or duck)

$^1/_2$ teaspoon garlic powder

$^1/_2$ teaspoon dried rosemary

$^1/_4$ cup chopped alfalfa sprouts

1 tablespoon chopped fresh parsley

$^1/_4$ cup yogurt

$^1/_4$ cup grated carrot

Melt the butter in a skillet over medium heat. Sauté the liver, turning frequently until lightly browned on all sides. Add the garlic powder and rosemary, then turn off the heat and cool to room temperature. Transfer to a food processor, add the alfalfa sprouts, parsley, yogurt, and carrot, and pulse until thick and creamy.

How to Grow Alfalfa Sprouts

To make your own alfalfa sprouts, place 2 tablespoons of alfalfa seeds (or red clover seeds) and 6 tablespoons of springwater in a half-gallon or gallon glass jar. Cover the jar with a sprouting screen or cheesecloth and soak seeds for six hours. Drain well, rinse and drain again, then cover the jar with a paper bag or cloth as the sprouts need a dark area at first; a closet is actually ideal. For the next three days, rinse and drain once in the morning and once in the evening. After three days, place the jar in a cool place with indirect sunlight to bring on the chlorophyll. Continue rinsing twice daily until you see bright green leaves. The sprouts are now ready for you or your pet to eat. Enjoy!

WHEATGRASS AND BARLEY GRASS

Bright emerald green and packed with nutrients, wheatgrass and barley grass are almost identical in their nutritional makeup and therapeutic properties. Some people claim that barley grass is much better at scavenging for free radicals and that wheatgrass has an edge in cancer prevention. In any case, both are excellent for reducing inflammation and pain. In their youth, before they grow into amber waves of grain and lose their chlorophyll potency, they contain nearly 90 percent of the minerals found in rich soil, along with large amounts of vitamins C, A, B_1, B_2, B_6, E, biotin, folic acid, choline, pantothenic acid, nicotinic acid, iron, potassium, calcium, magnesium, manganese, zinc, proteins, and enzymes—a proverbial mouthful. Their hundreds of enzymes, which are rarely available in such high concentrations in other foods, aid in digestion and assist the immune system by helping to destroy toxic substances in the body.

People and pets with allergies to wheat and other cereals are almost never allergic or sensitive to wheatgrass in its young, green stage. Some pets enjoy chewing on the grass itself, while others might need a pinch here and there—snuck in a shake or added to their stew. While fresh grass is best if you can get it (or grow it), dried and powdered forms are readily available, as is barley juice, my personal favorite. To understand just how vital greens are, consider the story of Larry and Buddy.

Larry and Buddy: Splendor in the Grass

Larry loved Buddy, his lumbering, four-year-old English sheepdog, but he couldn't figure out why Buddy would run hysterically through the park, stop to eat grass for a good twenty minutes, and then proceed to throw up. "He must need to vomit," Larry told me at a seminar I was giving at the Whole Foods Market in Las Vegas, Nevada.

I explained that most pets that eat potted plants or grass are simply trying to tell us that their bodies crave greens. Real greens are rarely found in commercial pet foods, but pets' bodies need them to process meats through the system most effectively; the enzymes in green foods helps break down the protein. Out in the wild, a predatory animal might consume a bird, a rabbit, or a lizard, along with its stomach contents, which would contain vegetable matter that the prey had eaten. I recommended that Larry give Buddy my own green food supplement containing barley grass juice powder, alfalfa juice powder, and other healthy herbs, plants, and berries.

Since most pets really enjoy the taste of green foods added to their meals, it was easy to understand why Buddy was to eager to receive the Vita-Dreams Daily Greens tablets, which Larry found right there in the store. Because greens absorb into the system so quickly, Larry noticed changes in Buddy's stamina levels in just a few days, and the vomiting ceased entirely.

Larry says that their jaunts to the park now consist of running, fetching, and stopping to smell the roses. Although Buddy takes splendor in the grass, he never eats it!

This recipe calls for barley juice powder, available in many health food stores. This nutritious, alkaline substance contains a nutrient-dense profile of vitamins, minerals, antioxidants, amino acids, enzymes, and chlorophyll.

The Color Green

Green symbolizes the onset of spring, bringing renewal and change. In Vedic teachings, the heart chakra is green, and it is the color most often associated with energy and serenity. Green is used in color therapy to calm and balance nerves, muscles, and thoughts. It works on the immune system and blood circulation, and is said to aid in prosperity, symbolizing great wealth and health. Some schools of thought connect the color green to our highest intelligence. No wonder green foods are an important element in anyone's diet—pet or human!

GREEN PÂTÉ

Yield: 45 servings / Serving Size: 1 tablespoon

$1/2$ cup coarsely chopped carrots

$1/4$ cup coarsely chopped yellow squash

$1/4$ cup coarsely chopped sweet potato

$1/2$ cup coarsely chopped green beans

$1/2$ cup green peas

$1/2$ cup coarsely chopped pumpkin

$1/4$ cup unsweetened berry juice

1 tablespoon barley juice powder

2 tablespoons grated Parmesan cheese

3 tablespoons plain yogurt

Mix all of the ingredients in a food processor until creamy. Serve on crackers. The pâté may be stored in a glass container in the refrigerator for up to 4 days.

SPIRULINA AND CHLORELLA

Spirulina and chlorella are both super sources of vitamins, minerals, protein, and antioxidants, and they're also a more concentrated source of chlorophyll than any other food. Although often lumped together, spirulina is a blue-green algae whereas chlorella is a green algae. But no matter how you classify them, both of these mighty single-celled organisms are excellent for digestion and nutrient absorption and are the key to preventive health for your animals. Spirulina is easy to digest and absorb, especially its protein. Although beef is only roughly 20 percent digestible, spirulina clocks in at a whopping 85 percent. Spirulina nurtures, tones, and cleanses the body, and it's particularly important for pets on the mend because it protects the kidneys from the damaging effects of prescription medications. Its healing powers are becoming legendary, especially as recent research suggests it can prevent viruses from entering human cells, as in HIV. Since feline immunodeficiency virus (FIV) is similar to the AIDS virus in humans, it's not far-fetched to assume spirulina could be an important addition to any cat's diet.

Chlorella has less protein than spirulina, but twice the nucleic acids and chlorophyll. That's why it's considered one of the best supplements for helping prevent cancer and tumors. Both of these algae help protect the liver from toxins, reduce blood pressure and cholesterol, fight free radicals, and reduce inflammation, not to mention that they're also rich in essential fatty acids.

Because they're so nutritionally dense, either spirulina or chlorella makes some pets hyperactive. As with all supplements (and even dietary changes), monitor how your pets react and make modifications as needed. If they seem beneficial but give your pet a lot of energy, you may want to supplement in the morning so you don't run the risk of your best friend inadvertently keeping you up all night.

> **"In blue-green algae such as spirulina,
> we find three and one-half billion years of life on
> this planet encoded in their nucleic acids (RNA/DNA).
> At the same time, all micro-algae supply that fresh
> burst of primal essence that manifested when life
> was in its birthing stages."**
>
> —PAUL PITCHFORD, author of *Healing with Whole Foods*

Week Four Assessment

❑ Have you identified all of the chemicals used on your lawn and garden? Have you made any changes or taken any precautions because of them?

❑ Did you use the list at the beginning of the chapter, along with other resources, to ensure that all of the plants in and around your home are safe for your pets? If any of your plants were unsafe, what did you do about it?

❑ If your dog or cat used to eat household plants or grass, after this week of added green foods it shouldn't be craving greens outside its food bowl. What changes have you observed?

❑ Have you bought any live sprouts, or are you starting a healthy sprout garden of your own?

❑ Have you noticed an increase in your pet's energy level?

Daily Play

Since it's likely that your pet's energy level has increased dramatically by this point, you can kick up its play a notch or two. If you can't squeeze in some extra activities during the week, make sure you add quality time on the weekends. I give my dogs at least one hour of swim time at the beach every week. They love fetching their floating rubber sticks, even in sixty-degree water.

Cat Play Tip: Make nutrition a part of your play dates with a vitamin chase. My cats love to chase their green vitamins across the floor. I make them work hard for their yummy treats, and they seem to enjoy them even more because of that. Chasing, capturing, and "killing" their vitamins always brings out the "beast" in them.

Dog Play Tip: Figure out what kind of toys your dog most likes to play with. Jasmine, my rambunctious six-year-old Australian shepherd, loves a plush, squeaky spider that makes lots of different sounds. I can throw it for hours and she'll always bring it back with wild enthusiasm. Make sure you don't play too rough, or the toys will tear and fall apart.

◆ ◆ ◆

You're now midway through the eight-week plan. Your pet's diet includes fresh, nourishing main meals and snacks enhanced with essential fatty acids and live green foods. You've got a daily play routine going, and chances are you're playing more and for longer sessions. Next week, you'll learn about B vitamins and how critical they are for physical health and emotional well-being. As you tune into any behavioral problems your pet may have, you'll begin to make the connection between those behaviors and any disharmony or stress in your household. When you begin to see your pet's moods as a reflection of your own, both of you will benefit.

CHAPTER SEVEN

Week Five: The Art of Well B-ing

In your journal:

- Complete your second Whole Pet Portrait. You and your pet are halfway through the program!

- Schedule your daily play dates.

- Throughout the week, fill in the Week at a Glance.

- At week's end, complete the Weekly Assessment.

Vitamins are essential nutrients that perform specific and vital functions necessary for maintaining health. The amount needed may be small, but the source or quality can have a huge impact on how effective they are in the body. This week we'll work with the water-soluble B vitamins and discover their benefits and uses. Because they're water-soluble, they easily leach out of foods during storage or preparation, and they also can't be stockpiled by the body. So daily supplementation is very important. (There is an upside to this, though; it's nearly impossible to overdo it when supplementing B vitamins because any excess is flushed out of the system.) We'll add sources of B vitamins, including Anitra Frazier's Vita-Mineral Mix, to your pet's food to replicate what your pet would eat in the wild.

The influence of the B vitamins is reflected both inside and outside the body. They help the body mine food for energy and increase stamina, and they're important for good vision, healthy skin, a gorgeous coat, calming the nervous system, and reducing anxiety and depression. They also help maintain precise communication between the nervous system and the brain. All of the B complex vitamins are important for the liver, muscles, brain, and red blood cell formation. Think of them collectively as one vitamin and always supplement them together, preferably in the form of nutritional yeast. As you'll learn later in this chapter, nutritional yeast is a good source for all of the B vitamins.

This chapter also covers a couple of other Bs—behavior and bran—behavior being linked to the Bs because of B complex's ability to support mental and emotional health and stability, and bran being an important component of Anitra Frazier's Vita-Mineral Mix, a great source of Bs and well-being. I also like to think of the B in B vitamins as standing for "blessings," because they truly do contribute to the happiness and tranquility of our animals, and surround them with an aura of glowing calmness, serenity, and greater well-being.

What to Expect

Glowing great health. A more supple coat. Healthier nails and teeth. Formerly timid or anxious pets will be calmer. Because your pet's body is beginning to eliminate toxins, much of the shedding and dandruff will have subsided. Hairballs should become a thing of the past and bowel movements or irregularities of the digestive tract should be less of an issue. Your pet is now well on its way toward true wellness.

Your Midpoint Whole Pet Portrait

You and your pet are halfway through the Whole Pet Diet program, and I'm guessing that you're witnessing some amazing changes. I'll bet your friends are noticing that your pet is becoming healthier, and because they don't see your pet every day, the results are even more obvious to them.

Take some time now to fill out your second Whole Pet Portrait. Fill out the form in your journal and take another picture or shoot some more video. Try to capture the essence of who your pet is today and how much better it's feeling than it did four weeks ago. Don't forget to zoom in for close-ups and focus special attention on the areas you were most concerned about when you started. It's likely that you'll see even more rapid improvement as you move through the rest of the program.

Project: Vita-Mineral Mix

This week I'd like you to make a batch of Anitra Frazier's Vita-Mineral Mix—for yourself as well as for your pets. You may ask, "Why me?" Well, are you stressed at work? Do your skin and nails appear dry, or do you feel you need to use extra conditioner or other products to make your hair shine? Anitra and I both use her Vita-Mineral Mix for these very reasons after seeing what it did for our pets. You can find all the ingredients at your local health food store. (Or if you're short on time, you can ask for the Vita-Mineral Mix product by name and purchase it premade.) Add the mix to your pet's food, and also blend it into your own smoothies, juices, soups, and stews. Try it for one week and you'll see visible differences in your own hair, your fingernails, and even the whites of your eyes—not to mention the calming effect on your nerves, which will naturally extend to and complement the emotional well-being of your pet. I recommend using it in uncooked dishes or adding it after cooking; it's most nutritious and most easily absorbed in its raw food form.

"A note on yeast and allergies:
some people think that yeast should not be
used as food for animals because it may cause
allergies. I can only report that my experience
is to the contrary. I find that yeast is an excellent
food without any such side effects."

—RICHARD PITCAIRN, DVM, author of
Dr. Pitcairn's Complete Guide to Natural Health for Dogs and Cats

B RAW: THE PURPOSE OF VITA-MINERAL MIX

Whether you feed your pet fresh or defrosted meat in your slow-cooked meals, it cannot duplicate all the nutrients of something freshly killed. Animals hunting in the wild consume everything—hair, bones, whiskers, and whatever's in the stomach of their prey—and the meat is still pulsing with life; there is simply no way that a domesticated diet can provide the same complement of nutrients and energy. But we can try our best to give our pets the nutrients they're missing out on, and that's why Anitra Frazier developed her Vita-Mineral Mix. Although she designed this supplement for cats, it's excellent for dogs, too. In her book *The New Natural Cat*, she explains the rationale behind her ingredients. She uses wheat bran to simulate rodents' stomach contents. Wheat bran, combined with kelp or mixed trace elements, supplies minerals and roughage similar to the prey's fur. Yeast, a living food, is a source of vital energy, and it also replaces some of the amino acids and B vitamins lost when foods are cooked, whether in homemade or canned foods.

Her recipe also contains lecithin (also known as phosphatidyl-choline), an important substance in cell membranes and the nervous system. Lecithin is thought to support the circulatory system and help lower cholesterol, probably due to its ability to emulsify fats; it helps eliminate chronic greasy coat syndrome. Lecithin is also the best known source of choline, which is found in every cell in the body and has its own long list of functions in the body. Most notably, it's essential for proper functioning of the liver and nervous system and it's a critical component of the neurotransmitter acetylcholine. All in all, it helps soothe the nerves of a high-strung or stressed-out pet.

Running a close second to EFAs (see chapter 3), Vita-Mineral Mix is great for eliminating hairballs and other accumulated materials in the digestive tract. The bran helps to flush out the entire system and remove any debris that may be blocking your pet up. Don't be fooled by synthetic petroleum-based hairball remedies or hairball-formula cat food. Most of these products contain mineral oil, which depletes the body of important vitamins A, D, and E, and can lead to major immune deficiency disorders. With all its nutritional benefits, Vita-Mineral Mix is a much better choice. This recipe makes a lot, so if you want to try it before making a full batch, just halve all of the ingredients.

ANITRA FRAZIER'S VITA-MINERAL MIX

Yield: About 7 cups / Serving Size: See below

1^1/$_2$ cups yeast powder (any food yeast—brewer's, torula, or nutritional)

^{1}/$_4$ cup kelp powder or mixed trace mineral powder

1 cup lecithin granules

2 cups wheat bran

2 cups calcium lactate or calcium gluconate

Mix all of the ingredients together and store in the refrigerator in a covered container. (Everything except the lecithin and minerals is perishable at room temperature.) Because Anitra's Vita-Mineral Mix contains bran (which acts like a tiny sponge), it's important to mix it with a little water before adding it to your pet's meal, as the yeast expands when it's wet. Use the table below to figure out how much of the supplement to mix into each meal and how much water to mix with it.

PET'S WEIGHT		AMOUNT OF VITA-MINERAL MIX		AMOUNT OF WATER
Up to 5 pounds	—	^{1}/$_2$ to 1 teaspoon	—	2 teaspoons
6 to 10 pounds	—	^{3}/$_4$ to 1^1/$_2$ teaspoons	—	3 teaspoons
11 to 20 pounds	—	1 to 2 teaspoons	—	4 teaspoons
21 to 40 pounds	—	2 to 3 teaspoons	—	5 teaspoons
41 to 80 pounds	—	3 to 4 teaspoons	—	2 tablespoons
Over 80 pounds	—	4 to 6 teaspoons	—	2^1/$_3$ tablespoons

B Complex: The Secret to Overall Well B-ing

There are eight water-soluble vitamins that primarily make up the B complex group: thiamine (B_1), riboflavin (B_2), niacin (B_3), pantothenic acid (B_5), pyridoxine (B_6), biotin (B_7), folic acid (B_9), and cyanocobalamin (B_{12}). These vitamins are found in many foods, and their positive influences are felt in nearly every part of the body. For supplementing the entire B complex, I highly recommend Anitra Frazier's mix over any B vitamin tablet because it's easier for the body to digest and assimilate. Its source of B vitamins is food yeast, which is one of the best immune-enhancing supplements available in food form.

Thiamine (B_1): Every cell in your pet's body needs thiamine because it helps release and transport energy from food. B_1 improves circulation, brain activity, and mental alertness; strengthens the muscles of the heart, stomach, and intestines; and assists in blood formation. A mood enhancer, it also wards off stinging insects and controls motion sickness. It can be found in pork, liver, and most meats, as well as whole grains, enriched grain products, peas, nutritional yeast, and legumes.

Riboflavin (B_2): Riboflavin aids in energy production and the metabolism of carbohydrates and fats. It promotes healthy skin and good vision (and may help with cataracts). It also protects against drug toxicity and environmental chemicals. Deficiencies of B_2 can lead to inflammation of the skin. Good food sources include liver, nutritional yeast, yogurt, cheese, fish, egg yolk, leafy green vegetables, alfalfa, chamomile, ginseng, red clover, broccoli, and wild rice.

Niacin (B_3): Niacin aids in digestion, lowers cholesterol levels and other types of fats in the blood, enhances memory, and helps with the synthesis of estrogen, testosterone, and other sex hormones. Signs of niacin deficiency include skin disorders, diarrhea, weakness, mental confusion, and irritability. Good sources include nutritional yeast, seeds, liver, fish, poultry, peanuts, and whole and enriched grain products. *Note:* Too much niacin can negatively affect the liver.

Pantothenic Acid (B$_5$): This calming vitamin increases stamina but also helps reduce anxiety, relieve depression, and maintain communication between the nervous system and the brain. Critical to many body functions, it assists in the breakdown of carbohydrates, fats, and proteins. This vitamin is also a component of coenzyme A, which is essential for metabolism. It's good for muscle cramping and can help calm a pet and reduce the side effects of drugs after surgery. Good food sources include nutritional yeast, yams, eggs, vegetables, organ meats, whole wheat, rice, wheat bran, mushrooms, and saltwater fish.

Pyridoxine (B$_6$): This vitamin is essential for protein metabolism and absorption, and therefore very important for cats, as they have a greater need for protein in their diet. B$_6$ plays an important role in physical and mental health, is key to red blood cell production and immune system performance, and is wonderful for the heart. You'll find it in bananas, nutritional yeast, sunflower seeds, wheat germ, soybeans, walnuts, broccoli, spinach, carrots, whole grains, potatoes, and alfalfa.

Biotin (B$_7$): Usually classified as a member of the B complex, biotin helps release energy from carbohydrates, fats, and proteins. It aids in cell growth and helps the body use other B vitamins. Biotin is essential to healthy coat and skin and eases muscle pain. It's especially important for anyone taking antibiotics, or for a pet with diabetes. Deficiencies can cause unhealthy weight loss and vomiting. Good sources include nutritional yeast, cheese, poultry, sea vegetables, yogurt, organ meats, sardines, and cooked egg whites. I stress *cooked* egg whites because raw egg whites may actually cause a deficiency in biotin.

Folic Acid (B$_9$): Also known as folate, this B vitamin boosts immunity and helps the nervous system perform at its peak. It can be found in nutritional yeast, brown rice, beef liver, salmon, tuna, poultry, peas, soybeans, dark leafy greens, and oranges.

Cyanocobalamin (B$_{12}$): This vitamin is said to be involved in every single immune system response, and studies show it's helpful against cancer and tumor formation. B$_{12}$ is only found in animal products: meats, liver, kidney, fish, oysters and other shellfish, eggs, and milk and milk products. Supplementation is exceedingly important for dogs on a vegetarian diet. Anemia is one of the first signs of a diet lacking in B_{12}.

B Is Nature's Tranquilizer

I often receive calls from distressed pet owners whose pets are acting depressed or exhibiting bad behavior. It breaks my heart to hear they're considering or have already turned to tranquilizers and drugs. Imagine prescribing Valium or Xanax for a pet with anxiety! Or how about giving Ritalin to a dog "diagnosed" with attention-deficit disorder? What is the world coming to? We're drugging the symptoms instead of addressing their causes, which may very well be the need for a healthier diet and a little more exercise and sunshine. In my opinion, the drug companies have taken the veterinarians a little too far here. There are plenty of natural approaches you can use to help your pet through all kinds of stress.

When people report behavioral problems in their pets, I always recommend that they first check their pet's food to see whether it contains chemicals and preservatives. These artificial ingredients are often highly antagonistic and can actually contribute to an animal's mental and emotional imbalance. Some additives can be so detrimental that they can actually have the same effect on a pet as hallucinogenic drugs have on people. According to Best Friends Animal Shelter, the famous no-kill shelter in Kanab, Utah, the most common reason pets are put down by vets or turned into shelters is because of unruly behavior. Instead of throwing up our hands and giving up on these potentially great creatures, who depend on us for their very lives, it's time to take a whole pet approach and change their diet and living conditions. In that vein, there's much to be said about the benefits of adding vitamins, particularly the full complex of B vitamins, and minerals to a pet's food to help with behavior problems.

Be aware that any situation that causes you duress can also trigger stress in your pet. Beyond that, it's important to look at your pet's world from its point of view. Keep in mind that cats and dogs are creatures of habit; anything that upsets their normal routine or invades their territory is taxing, if not traumatic. Here are some of the primary stressors for pets:

- Loss of a companion, animal or human

- Absence of family members, animal or human

- New environments

- Introduction of a new pet

- Extreme changes in the household routine

- A trip to the vet or groomer

- A stressed owner

A friend recently moved from a large house to a small apartment with her two cats. She told me that one cat hid in the closet or stared at the walls, two obvious signs of fear or depression. The other cat became disruptive and continuously voiced his displeasure by knocking things off tables and creating chaos in the kitchen. The new, smaller space had only one litter box, and both cats became territorial. Part of the solution in this case was to add another litter box and create more quality time with each cat individually. Although supplementing with B vitamins helped alleviate symptoms, it took a well-rounded holistic approach to bring balance to the household.

B Positive—Pets Are Emotional Sponges

As my friend's story shows, food and supplements are important to your pet's well-being, but positive surroundings and a healthy emotional environment are equally important. Dogs, cats, birds, and other creatures we bring into our world are tuned in to all of our different moods and stresses. Your pet reflects you, and it's possible that disease or debilitation in your life can be transferred to your pet. Conversely, by keeping a positive mental attitude, you can help your pet achieve better health more quickly. This is all the more reason to keep your chin up, maintain a positive attitude, and try to remain calm. It's healthier for you, and it will benefit your pet.

Think about this: every time you get home, your pet is ever so eager to greet you. Most pet owners enjoy the wildly ecstatic "yippee, my people are finally home!" routine when they are welcomed in with wagging tails, barks of joy, jumping, prancing, or purring. Even if you've had a bad day, your sweet companion helps mend a stressful situation or a disappointment and lends a paw to assist you toward recovery with its joy. It's critical to acknowledge your pet's celebration of life with lots of encouraging praise, a few healthy treats, or a trip down the street with a favorite toy to unleash some of that pent-up excitement.

I think that the more positive attention and sense of routine we give our pets, the better we support them. It's a full circle of love that helps us stay healthier, too. Sometimes it's easier to make and keep our pets well than it is to work on transforming our own lives, but like ripples in a pond, the changes you make to support your pet's health will probably touch and support your own health and happiness. And isn't it worth some effort to help your beloved pet achieve optimal health and emotional well-being? After all, who else loves you so unconditionally?

When you need help relieving your pet's stress, instead of turning to medications, look into the alternative therapies or natural substances that can contribute positively to its emotional state. Of course, love and spending quality time with you top the list of antistress treatments, and a high-quality diet is essential for supporting any treatment you choose. Beyond those fundamentals, also consider a calming massage along with positive conversation with your pet. It's important to continuously reassure your pet that all is well.

Rescue Remedy—Good for You, Good for Your Pet

When a pet is under stress, it's pretty safe to assume that the rest of the household may be stressed, too. In times of trouble or trauma, I often reach for my Rescue Remedy, the most popular of the Bach Flower Remedies. This particular remedy is a safe and soothing blend of natural feel-good flower essences that can be administered in the pet's water or directly by dropper into the mouth as needed. It's made for people, but it works well for animals, too. According to Dr. Edward Bach, this combination of five different flower essences helps people (or their pets) cope better in emergencies or stressful events. Dr. Bach believed that treating the feelings and personalities of patients is as important as treating their physical ailments. He found that by addressing emotions, moods, and mental tendencies, when unhappiness and physical distress were alleviated, the body's natural healing potential became unblocked and the immune system kicked in and performed at a higher level, allowing the body to heal itself in its numerous ways. I have used Rescue Remedy many times over the years; it can be administered orally in its concentrated form or diluted in water. Since you can't overuse it, sometimes I reach for it several times daily. A few drops for me, a few drops for my sometimes hyper dog, Jasmine! In addition to the Bach products, Dr. Goodpet makes a comparable line for animals. Both products can be found in health food stores or online.

B Open-Minded and Listen to Your Pet

In the book *Good Dogs, Bad Habits*, Ranny Green explains that most dogs with behavior issues are actually good dogs, but they haven't had the proper training and reinforcement to be the best they can be. In *The New Natural Cat*, Anitra Frazier reminds us that cats with behavior problems are "not trying to get back at their owners" but may instead have medical problems that need attention. Our pets are always trying to tell us something, and Voyko and I have learned over the years that if you just open your mind and listen, you'll get what you need to help put your pet (and hopefully yourself) back on the path to wellness.

Sometimes it just takes time, a step back, the addition of supplements, and a desire to learn. I experienced this once with a dog who at first seemed beyond help.

Sweetie: A Damaged Life Worth Saving

When I arrived at the office early one morning with my dog Bravo by my side, I found half my staff scurrying around the business park frantically trying to capture a very large, wild-eyed, white stray dog. She was lost, wounded, and bound for disaster if she wasn't confined in a hurry. This poor creature radiated fear and mistrust and couldn't be lured with calm words or even the yummiest treats. As her eyes darted in every direction, we could see how afraid she was, and keeping her out of harm's way was proving difficult with cars zooming by from every side street. When she spotted Bravo (who was always a great bitch magnet), she ran straight to him, seeking shelter from another of her kind. My sensitive boy calmed and consoled her, and within a few minutes we had her contained and the crisis seemed over.

At first we tried to find her owners: hundreds of posters went up, and we notified all the local shelters that we had found a very unusual dog. Pure white, she had the head and body of a golden retriever and the coat and tail of an American Eskimo. I thought someone would surely be missing her, but as I started to observe her more, it occurred to me that I could never send her back to where she came from.

Sadly, this dog had obviously been beaten and abused, and she shook uncontrollably when anyone approached her. She was covered in ticks and bleeding vaginally from being in heat, and her long white coat was terribly matted. I felt certain she was used only for breeding, and it was apparent that she'd had many litters of pups, all recently. This pitiful dog was horribly underweight and mal-nourished, yet she refused any food or water for several days. She lacked social skills and seemed petrified to set foot in our home, but she was seemingly too weak to resist our care. So we gave her a warm, snug place to sleep with a view of the rest of the curious household (which included Bravo and his Aussie sister, Jasmine, along with a very roost-ruling cat named Kitty). Initially, our new houseguest refused Voyko's wonderful home-cooked meals with lots of fresh meat (protein is brain food), but after two days, the strong aroma of his delicious fare broke through her resistance. She finally began to trust us enough to take food, provided no one was looking. It broke our hearts to see such a magnificent creature so confused and frightened. We named her Sweetie in the hopes that she would grow into her name and fit nicely into our household.

As Sweetie got stronger, she sought the attention of the other dogs, although she wouldn't actually play with them. Play had no place in her prior life, which was probably full of physical and emotional stresses stemming from caring for all of her litters under less-than-ideal conditions. Slowly we won her trust. Though her skin was quite tender, she loved the feel of a light, gentle brushing. She cleaned up beautifully with botanical shampoos and peppermint spritzes, which also fended off ticks. And as soon as we could, we had her spayed.

As we gave her supplements and fed her great food fortified with Anitra's Vita-Mineral Mix and fresh herbs, she began to heal physically and she seemed to gain strength daily. But the emotional and mental part took longer to solve. To our dismay and frustration, every time she went outside a crazed look came over her face and she bolted off the property, fleeing from the imaginary demons that still haunted her. Time and again we sent search parties out, and we started to worry that's we'd never be able to trust her off leash. The hardest part was mustering the emotional energy to welcome her back with happy voices and praise each time she came back home. It took eighteen months before she stopped running away.

Time, patience, nutritious food, and wisdom eventually created a healthy and magnificent creature. We all learned how to "raise with

*praise" more effectively, and Voyko and I promised each other to fill
our home with positive energy to support the entire family. Sweetie
finally found peace and a loving environment, and she gets a lot of
satisfaction from her job of guarding the house every day. She's
gained much so confidence and has grown so statuesque that she
is currently pursuing an exciting career in modeling and greets
adoring fans all over the world.*

Health Is More Than Skin-Deep

Dandruff, an oily coat, or a greasy tail is an outward sign that your pet
is trying to rid itself of toxins and may have more serious inner problems. Treating these skin and coat issues with topical shampoos isn't
going to get to the root of the problem. The skin is the largest organ
of the body and has many functions. It protects your pet from heat,
cold, and injuries, helps regulate body temperature, is often the first
defense against infection, and is important to sensory perception, giving your pet a lot of information about its surroundings. The skin is
also part of your pet's elimination system. A little oil is normal, but too
much oil, manifesting as an oily coat and greasy tail, could mean your
pet has a waste disposal problem related to its kidneys or liver.

Similar concepts apply to dandruff. The skin continuously sheds
dead cells as part of its normal rejuvenation process, but excessive
shedding of dead skin cells in the form of dandruff is abnormal and
indicates disorder or imbalance in the body. The skin must be well
nourished to stay healthy, and essential fatty acids are especially important to this end. Without them, dandruff, dry skin, and itching abound.
The B vitamins also play important roles in good skin condition
because they stimulate elimination and help the body dispose of waste
through the proper channels (pee and poop).

As I've mentioned before, outer health reflects inner health. Now
that you understand how critical it is to support good health from
within through diet, I'm sure you have a better sense of why a lifelong

diet of dry foods can lead to a myriad of problems. In addition to obvious external signs like dry skin and coat, skin diseases, excessive shedding, and dandruff, these problems include a long list of digestive disorders, from frequent vomiting to irritable bowel syndrome and constipation. I often liken a pet's digestive system to a kitchen sink and plumbing. When you first move into a new home, the plumbing always works well. Over time, as you put food and waste down the drain, eventually you wind up with plumbing problems and you may need to resort to chemicals or a professional plumber with a mechanical snake. As debris collects inside the pipes, it gradually builds up a residue (or a plaque) that ultimately needs to be removed to allow the system to flow freely. Bodies, whether of pets or people, are very similar. All the indigestible foods tend to clog the body as well. Dry food heads the list of foods that your pet can't easily absorb, utilize, or eliminate.

Dry food was certainly the culprit in the plight of Magnolia, the cat of a staff member at Halo.

Magnolia: Moving in the Right Direction

Cheryl had always accepted the veterinarian's explanation that Magnolia was "just fine." He told her that all cats throw up regularly, and that it's quite normal. For twelve years, Cheryl diligently purchased what she thought was the best dry food for her petite and delicate tabby until she came to work for Halo, Purely for Pets. I always ask new employees if there's something about their pet they'd like to see change; this way they can experience the company's philosophy and products firsthand. Cheryl didn't have to think twice; she was so ready to be done with the daily vomiting routine and the ritual of scooping up those slimy hairballs from her otherwise clean floors. I told her that although Magnolia's digestive woes might be the norm, they certainly weren't normal, and that I was quite certain the right food and supplements would help Magnolia.

Eager for change, Cheryl put Magnolia on our chicken stew and Anitra's Vita-Mineral Mix. Over the course of three weeks, Magnolia's coat became healthier. She stopped shedding excessively, allowing her to stop ingesting all that loose, dead hair when she groomed herself. To Cheryl's amazement, she no longer found any more piles of regurgitated fur and cat food on the floor. But Cheryl felt even better that Magnolia was finally absorbing and utilizing nutrients from the food she now swore to serve every day. Life is happier when everything moves in the proper direction, and the introduction of bran, B vitamins, and other healthy foods contributed enormously to Magnolia's obvious well B-ing.

Week Five Assessment

❑ How did it go making and using Anitra's Vita-Mineral Mix? Were you able to find all the ingredients?

❑ Did you add it only to your pet's food, or did you also try it yourself? How did you serve it? What results have you noticed?

❑ Are there any unresolved skin or coat issues? Have digestive issues settled down, including hairballs?

❑ How about any behavioral issues in your pet, such as nervousness? Can you identify what creates stressful situations in your household? Are you stepping back far enough to examine everything that may be a little out of balance, including yourself? Are you aware of how your pet absorbs your emotions, acting as a reflection of you?

❑ Have you gotten a bottle of Rescue Remedy for those times when you both may need it?

❑ Are you creating simple routines in the house to help instill balance? What are you discovering about your pet that you hadn't noticed before?

Daily Play

By now, you should be doing two play sessions each day with your pet, for at least ten minutes each, if not fifteen minutes each. Here are a few more tips for pet play.

Cat Play Tip: High jumps are great exercise for a cat, and a very natural movement. Try getting your cat to jump up on a scratching post, a window ledge, or a stool for a treat. Yes, this does count as moving, stretching, and jumping! Or take a long peacock feather and tease your cat into chasing it along the floor and up into the air. This exercise is likely to go on for as long as you're willing keep going, providing endless fun for the two of you.

Dog Play Tip: Dogs love Frisbees, and you can even use a soft, Nerf-type Frisbee in the house. If your dog doesn't play with a Frisbee, start offering food and treats in a Frisbee upside down to get your dog used to going for it. Soon you can roll it across the floor and your dog will chase it, and from there it's just a matter of finding space and perfecting your style.

◆ ◆ ◆

The B vitamin complex took the spotlight this week, a great healer for any skin, coat, and digestive disorders and emotional distress that may have been troubling your pet—or you. The B vitamins, bran, and minerals in the Vita-Mineral Mix are starting to work their magic, and you may even be seeing better behavior. In week six, we'll add the antioxidant properties of vitamins C, A, and E and the mineral selenium to your pet's diet. Your pet will also enjoy receiving a nurturing massage from you—sure to be the first of many sessions.

CHAPTER EIGHT

Week Six:
The Art of Immunity
and Healing Touch

In your journal:

- Complete the Weekly Checkup.

- Schedule your daily play dates.

- Throughout the week, fill in the Week at a Glance.

- At week's end, complete the Weekly Assessment.

This week we add vitamin C and three other antioxidants, vitamin A, vitamin E, and selenium, which make up your four "aces in the hole" to elevate your pet's immune system to optimal levels. Together, these give every cell of the body increased capacity to heal and ward off disease. You'll learn about many of the benefits of vitamin C, including its functions as an anti-inflammatory, antidepressant, and flu fighter. Vitamin C also supports the heart, calms the nerves, helps strengthen tooth enamel, and builds collagen in support of skin, tendon, bone, cartilage, and connective tissue. Vitamin C even helps fight the negative side effects of drugs and prescription medications. Think of this mighty vitamin as a guardian angel, fiercely protecting your pet from everything from common everyday stresses to potentially deadly diseases, including cancer. We'll also explore the healing power of massage for your pet.

What to Expect

A more youthful, more vital pet who can recover from or fend off illnesses much more easily. Your pet will also be calmer and more secure because of the connection you'll forge through gentle, loving massage. You'll see changes in yourself this week too, as you become more aware of and confident in your own ability to provide healing through massage. Since there are natural stresses that all pets experience during times of growth, recovery, or aging, you may find yourself shifting the ways you approach your pet.

Vitamin C, also known as ascorbic acid, is truly a miracle worker. It's critical for any animal, but especially those who have eaten commercial, pet-grade food for any length of time, because the chemical preservatives used in these foods can actually rob the body of large quantities of vitamin C, leaving pets vulnerable to and defenseless against infection and disease. Like the B vitamins, vitamin C is water-soluble, and because the body does not store it, the need for replacing it daily is paramount. Because it's easily leached out of foods during storage or preparation, supplements are a more reliable source. And because the body will excrete what it can't use in a fairly short period of time, you should give your pet vitamin C at intervals throughout the day.

Vitamin C operates at the cellular level and is important to nearly every bodily function. Besides working as an antioxidant to neutralize free radicals, which I'll get to later in this chapter, it's important to bone health, plays a major role in fighting infections, and promotes healing of tissues that are damaged and scarred, making it famous for its anti-aging properties. The real power of vitamin C is in its relationship to the immune system, where it fights free radicals and neutralizes toxic by-products of fat metabolism. This heroic substance has amazing therapeutic benefits for cats with feline lower urinary tract disease (FLUTD) and feline leukemia virus (FeLV). It's also important for aging pets and dogs with arthritis or hip dysplasia. In addition, vitamin C has been called "nature's aspirin" because it can ease pain caused by inflammation.

Project: Get in Touch with Your Pet

As you fortify your pet with the miraculous vitamin C this week, I want you to add the power of your own healing touch as well. Massage has many of the same benefits for pets as it does for humans. In addition to helping with sore muscles, chronic pain, and flexibility issues, it enhances circulation, bringing more blood and nutrients to problem areas and transporting toxins away. Beyond these and other physical benefits, massage helps reduce stress. And perhaps most importantly, taking this special time with your pet communicates your love and caring concern in a way that your pet can truly understand. With massage, you take power into your own healing hands.

Massaging your pet daily also gives you an opportunity to make important assessments. By putting emphasis on your own keen observations, you'll begin to actually feel the changes your pet has been undergoing in the last five weeks. I encourage you to touch each and every one of your pet's body parts each day this week, making mental notes of things that have shifted since you started on the program and then logging them into your Whole Pet Journal.

Since relaxation is key to successful therapeutic massage, never force the issue. If your pet is reluctant, scale back to simple petting motions, then gradually increase the pressure and your intention. Start by massaging your pet's head and studying its face, ears, eyes, and muzzle. Then move down to its neck and shoulders, and then to the rest of the body. Massage along your pet's spine and legs, and gently palpate its abdomen. "Pawlpate" its paws, too, if it will let you! Take about ten minutes to gently massage your pet's entire body. If you find any lumps, or if anything you do seems to cause your pet pain, back off and consider whether you've found something you should mention to your vet. Then, in your Whole Pet Journal, describe any changes that are taking place on your pet's coat, skin, belly, joints, legs, tail, and feet.

Now that you've taken power into your own healing hands, let's move on to the wonders of vitamin C.

The Buzz about Vitamin C

I first became a believer in vitamin C for pets twenty years ago, after devouring the book *How to Have a Healthier Dog*, by Wendell O. Belfield, DVM. At that time, Dr. Belfield had fifteen years of clinical experience, and after working with over two thousand animals he saw that dogs definitively benefit from extra vitamin C. Since then he's learned even more and now points out that dogs on a regimen of this vitamin are much less likely to develop hip dysplasia, spinal myelopathy, ruptured disks, viral diseases, and even skin problems. Anitra Frazier, the natural cat expert, was also an early exponent. Though healthy cats can make some vitamin C in their intestines, she reminds us that the operative words are *healthy* and *some*. Frazier emphasizes cats can only manufacture enough vitamin C if their diet is rich in all other essential nutrients. Commercial pet-grade foods don't provide the broad spectrum of naturally occurring nutrients to enable this, so it's unlikely that your cat is getting enough vitamin C on a diet of store-bought foods. Depletion of vitamin C leaves a cat or dog easy prey to every germ or virus that happens along.

> **"Ascorbic acid is absolutely essential to the living process and all living forms either produce it themselves or get it in their food, or they perish within three months. No other vitamin deficiency works that fast."**
>
> —WENDELL O. BELFIELD, DVM, author of *How to Have a Healthier Dog*

Getting Vitamin C into the Diet and Keeping It in the System

I have much more to say about the powers of vitamin C and its antioxidant partners in this chapter, but given what you've already learned, undoubtedly you're eager to start adding it to your pet's diet, so let's talk about how to do it. When you think of ascorbic acid, you probably think of oranges, grapefruit, lemons, and other citrus fruits, but vitamin C is abundant in vegetables and other fruits as well, especially broccoli, Brussels sprouts, cauliflower, cabbage, leafy green vegetables, acerola cherries, rose hips, watercress, parsley, black currants, strawberries, kiwifruit, guavas, and my personal favorite, super green barley grass juice, which is said to have seven times the amount of vitamin C found in an equivalent weight of oranges. (However, it's probably best to avoid feeding your pet cruciferous vegetables, such as broccoli, Brussels sprouts, cauliflower, and cabbage, or to use them only sparingly. Although they're rich in vitamins, they can cause gas.)

My pets don't care much for citrus fruits and their sour properties, so I artfully camouflage ascorbic acid in their favorite treats or mixed in well with their stew. (The acid taste is best neutralized by a protein.) I prefer a powder or a liquid vitamin C supplement, as most pets find the sour-tasting pills unacceptable and spit them out. I also question the dubious ingredients in a tablet, because in order for them to hold together they have to contain binders and fillers, which need not be listed on the label. In the development of my own powdered vitamin C supplement, I chose to use the potent white pulp of a variety of citrus fruits because they also provide bioflavonoids, which help the body absorb and utilize the naturally occurring vitamin C. I added acerola cherries and rose hips, which contain rutin and hesperidin and provide natural antiviral, anti-inflammatory, and antiallergy properties in a very absorbable form.

VITAMIN C DOSAGES

When supplementing vitamin C, consider splitting the daily recommendation into three or four doses per day. I recommend splitting a meal or a snack into two portions and serving them at different times to accommodate giving your pet vitamin C mixed into its food several times a day. By supplying more frequent doses, you ensure that your pet's body is provided with vitamin C for longer periods of time, enabling it to use as much as it possibly can. The doses below are for general maintenance. It's fine to double these dosages during times of stress or for overcoming specific ailments.

Pet's Weight	Amount of Vitamin C
2 to 10 pounds	— up to 625 mg per day
11 to 25 pounds	— up to 1,250 mg per day
26 to 50 pounds	— up to 2,500 mg per day
51 to 100 pounds	— up to 3,750 mg per day
Over 100 pounds	— up to 5,000 mg per day

Dosage Tip: Always start with a small amount of vitamin C and slowly increase the dose every few days until you work your way up to the ideal amount. Adding too much vitamin C all at once, before the body is used to it, may cause loose stools or an upset stomach.

CHOOSE VITAMIN C SUPPLEMENTS WITH CARE

Not all vitamins are created equal. If you're supplementing and not experiencing the results you expected, it might have something to do with the quality of the ingredients or the formulation. Become a conscientious label reader and scrutinize all ingredient lists and supplement facts panels. The purest form of vitamin C is natural ascorbic acid. There are many products on the market that contain other ingredients, such as calcium or sodium, which are used as buffering agents to reduce acidity. Because these supplements contain ingredients other than vitamin C, the manufacturers could actually be skimping on the amounts of vitamin C in the product.

I don't recommend sodium ascorbate because the added salt (sodium) can negate vitamin C's benefits by increasing your pet's risk of heart problems or other ailments. The calcium in calcium ascorbate might be equally problematic. The importance of creating a 2:1 ratio of calcium to phosphorous is very well documented, and the potential overuse of calcium could cause an imbalance in the system. Vitamin supplements should be deliberately chosen to specifically address your individual pet's needs.

Spud: The Miracle Cat

Spud was a sad little kitten, an at-risk pet at a Bide-A-Wee shelter. At-risk pets are typically too far gone to rehabilitate and have only slim chances of finding a home. Spud had an unusual look about her: black and white tufts of fur stuck out everywhere, and she had a big black rectangular patch centered directly over her mouth. Fortunately for Spud, Kay was determined to leave the shelter that day with a new kitten to love, and she kept returning to the cage where the "Groucho Marx look-alike" slept.

The shelter workers warned Kay that Spud had developed a respiratory infection and had the worst case of ear mites the vet had ever seen (Spud actually tore the tips off both ears). Plus, her liver was compromised and blood work indicated kidney disease. Undaunted by this catalog of complaints, Kay adopted Spud, along with her suitcase-sized box full of medications. Kay was religious about giving Spud her meds, and she brought Spud back to the shelter on a regular basis for injections to help with her liver—a lifelong necessity, or so she was told by the vet.

Spud had many bouts with ailments and was often forced to take a thick, pink liquid antibiotic, which Kay thought of as "Pepto Dismal." The cat would vomit regularly, and Kay spent many an hour cleaning sticky, pink puke off the walls. Although Spud gave Kay buckets of love, there was never a lapse in the stress of dealing with her ailments. For seven years, Spud was happy enough. She gained some much needed weight, mustered some kittenish energy, and had a choice of both dry and wet food, and while she was never considered a healthy cat, she certainly proved that love and attention do wonders for the soul. She enjoyed playing with her very own dog and sunning on the window perch with its expansive view.

One night, Kay realized she hadn't seen Spud since early that morning. She finally found her in a closet, and when she pried her out, Kay was horrified to see she was all skin and bones. A pinch on the back of the neck told her that Spud was completely dehydrated. First thing in the morning, away to the vet they went. Kay told the vet she noticed Spud urinating outside the litter box earlier that day, but that she thought the cat was simply unhappy about her long hours at work. After running some tests, the vet proclaimed that Spud's kidneys and liver were failing and that she'd developed jaundice, apparent in her eyes and skin. He quickly administered fluids to keep the severely dehydrated kitty alive, but he wasn't hopeful. Then he dropped the next bomb: if Spud's own organs didn't kill her, the negative side effects of all those medications could. He suggested it might be time to "put her to sleep."

But Kay had a different plan. She took Spud home and stopped all of her medications. What was meant to be would be. Kay understood how draining the stress was for both of them and recoiled from the notion of any more shots or medications. She realized the drugs had to be part and parcel of Spud's downfall. Kay had recently heard about the miracles of real foods and the power of vitamin C, so she decided to take an alternative, more natural approach. Anything was better than what they were doing now.

Kay started introducing my homemade stew into Spud's old food, gradually decreasing the old food until Spud was eating only the new, high-quality food. Since that transition went fairly well, Kay gained confidence about making even more changes. She added green foods and provided gradually increasing doses of vitamin C to help boost Spud's immune system and detoxify her poor little body from all of the chemicals she had consumed in her life. Kay was surprised at how quickly Spud seemed to improve, gaining energy and putting a few pounds onto her emaciated frame. And you can bet Spud was thrilled about no more pink liquids. To this day, Kay loves telling me how her vet recalls Spud as the "miracle cat." Over the next three years, the vet gave her no further treatments and proclaimed that her recovery and longevity were due to divine intervention. To me it was common sense. Kay simply says that she "let Spud's food be her medicine and her medicine be her food."

VITAMIN C FOR BLADDER HEALTH

Vitamin C is especially important for cats because it helps strengthen the urinary tract and bladder walls and helps destroy bacteria associated with feline lower urinary tract disease (FLUTD). (FLUTD used to be known as FUS, or feline urologic syndrome, but that term is confusing because it's used to describe almost all urinary tract disorders—everything from kidney and bladder stones to urinary blockage and cystitis.) FLUTD, a disease caused by stress and diet, is often associated with high urinary pH values (pH values basically run from 1 to 14, where 7 is neutral, anything lower is acidic, and anything higher is alkaline or basic). Cold, wet weather may also trigger FLUTD, especially during any stressful times in the household. Nutritionists, homeopaths, and holistic vets agree that a healthy homemade diet, rich in antioxidants, particularly vitamin C, will help acidify the urine, aid detoxification, and help boost the immune response.

Bladder and urinary diseases can become chronic problems for both dogs and cats, particularly if they're fed a steady diet of dry food. Dry food and even grain-based wet foods often create an extreme alkalinity in the urine, and this can cause the formation of magnesium ammonium phosphate crystals in cats and bladder stones in dogs. By increasing supplementation of vitamin C when symptoms appear, your pet's urine will stay slightly more acidic (as Mother Nature intends), alleviating these problems.

Dogs: Hip Dysplasia, Collagen, and Vitamin C

Hip dysplasia is a chronic, crippling, arthritic condition in dogs that attacks the hindquarters and can leave them debilitated, hunched up, and in pain. The problem begins as a result of the hip joint not forming properly. Large-breed dogs and their offspring are at the greatest risk, especially during their initial growth stages, when additional stress is placed on the bones and joints. Holistic veterinarians often recommend large doses (also called megadoses) of vitamin C during this critical phase.

The standard theory holds that inbreeding of large dogs has weakened the gene pool and left many of these purebreds predisposed to problems with physical development. Short-legged and long-backed breeds, such as dachshunds, corgis, and basset hounds, face similar challenges. The further a dog's body type diverges from resembling the natural form of the wolf, the greater the challenges they face, in both physiology and temperament.

But Wendell Belfield, DVM, doesn't agree with the view that hip dysplasia is often due to inbreeding or poor genetics. In fact, his study of eight litters of dysplastic German shepherds and their offspring convinced him that it's definitely biochemical. When mothers with hip dysplasia were given megadoses of vitamin C and their pups were kept on a maintenance regime throughout their period of fast growth, there were no signs of the crippling disease.

Without ascorbic acid, dogs' bodies can't produce the collagen necessary to support their bones. Collagen is the substance that pretty much keeps all animals in their specific forms. It provides structure to the body by protecting and supporting the softer tissues and connecting them with the skeleton. Without vitamin C, there is no collagen, and without collagen, there's no support for the tissues connecting the bones. So you can see why it's a necessary a nutrient for dogs with hip dysplasia or for any pet with arthritis. Two other supplements, glucosamine and chondroitin, are exceedingly helpful for arthritis and bone and joint problems, especially when used in conjunction with vitamin C. Their specific benefits and properties will be discussed in chapter 9.

ENVIRONMENTAL POLLUTION, VITAMIN C, AND FELINE LEUKEMIA

A strong, healthy immune system is the best defense against disease for any pet, but these days it's especially critical for cats. Feline leukemia, considered the most deadly and devastating of cat diseases, is spreading at alarming rates. This terrible disease attacks the white blood cells, compromising the immune system and causing lymphosarcoma or leukemia. Much like the AIDS virus in humans, it can be transmitted from one cat to another through bodily fluids. And since many cats carry the virus without displaying symptoms, they can transmit it to other cats without your ever suspecting what's going on.

The evidence that this disease is caused or complicated by environmental pollutants is overwhelming. Chemicals used directly on cats, such as flea and tick control products, as well as household cleaners, insecticides, and contaminants in drinking water, might very well be direct links to feline leukemia (and other health problems, too). Fortunately, as new information emerges, many diseases no longer carry a death sentence, including feline leukemia. With a holistic approach and a conscientious, concerted effort, it's possible to support the body in its ability to heal itself and keep the perpetrators at bay.

Every prominent holistic vet, nutritionist, and natural practitioner I know recommends a two-pronged approach to feline leukemia: strengthen the immune system with vitamin C and get rid of anything and everything in your pet's life that contributes to its weakness (two keystones of this eight-week plan you're following).

STRESS AND VITAMIN C

As I've already pointed out, pets are emotional sponges; they absorb our moods and feelings, positive or negative. Generally, any situation that causes you stress can trigger the same response in your pet, and stress can weaken the immune system. You can help calm your pet by supplementing with the full complex of B vitamins, and you also need to bolster its immune response with vitamin C. Cats and dogs do make some vitamin C in their bodies, but they require greater amounts in times of stress. It is said that some of the tremendous survival mechanisms of rats are related to their production of ascorbic acid, which increases to ten times its normal rate in response to stress. In the mammal hierarchy, dogs and cats are actually much lower on the totem pole in their abilities to produce vitamin C, and yet they burn it up just as quickly when stresses are present.

> **"It is not the cancer that kills the victim;**
> **it is the breakdown of the defense mechanism**
> **that eventually brings death."**
>
> —DR. HARDIN JONES, renowned cancer researcher, University of California

Antioxidants: For Prevention and Defense

The terms *free radicals* and *antioxidants* have been so overused that they sound like commercial hype, something designed to sell vitamins. But free radicals are a genuine health threat, and pets, just like humans, need antioxidants to combat them. In a process known as oxidation, free radicals, which are unstable, attack nearby stable molecules to "steal" electrons. The attacked molecule then becomes a free radical, and the ultimate result can be a chain reaction that can kill cells. On the one hand, free radicals are a normal by-product of metabolism and are formed during everyday functions, such as breathing and digesting. In fact, the immune system produces free radicals to fight invading bacteria and viruses. On the other hand, when free radicals are produced in large quantities, they can be extremely damaging. On top of that, other toxins in the environment, like cigarette smoke, air pollution, preservatives in food, and chemicals in drinking water, trigger free radical activity and accelerate their production. Free radicals are thought to play a major role in heart and lung disease, cancer, and cataracts, and there is growing evidence that damage caused by free radicals underlies the gradual deterioration in the aging process. We can minimize the impact of free radicals with antioxidants—substances that neutralize free radicals.

Antioxidants can put a stop to free radical chain reactions by "donating" an electron to the cause. They don't become free radicals themselves because they're still stable after donating an electron. Four of the best-known antioxidants found in nature are beta-carotene (a form of vitamin A), vitamin C, vitamin E, and the mineral selenium. Their acronym, ACES, is a great reminder that these are your "aces in the hole"—the best resource we have to help the immune system combat the aging process and most diseases. So let's take a closer look at your other three aces: vitamin A, vitamin E, and selenium.

Vitamin A: Important for good vision and reproduction, vitamin A also helps promotes healthy skin, hair, and bones. As a free radical scavenger, it helps prevent infections of the bladder, kidneys, and lungs. Holistic vets often use it in the treatments of epilepsy, FLUTD, feline leukemia, dermatitis, and inflammatory bowel disease. Carrots, pumpkin, squash, yams, and sweet potatoes are all excellent sources of beta-carotene, which is actually a double molecule of vitamin A. Cats have difficulty converting beta-carotene from plants into vitamin A, so they must obtain it from other sources, such as liver, yogurt, and cod liver oil.

Vitamin E: Often used in conjunction with vitamin C, this vitamin helps sweep up free radicals. Vitamin E is known as the "heart vitamin" because of its ability to significantly reduce heart disease in humans. It's also considered critically important in fighting cancer because it bolsters immune system response. It's good for skin, muscles, hair, nerves, and vision. It also helps to eliminate scar tissue, both externally and internally. Like vitamin A, it's recommended for pets with feline leukemia, epilepsy, and viral infections, and it's also used to treat mange in dogs. Good sources include dark leafy greens, whole grains, liver, green foods, alfalfa, rose hips, and soybeans. Vitamin E is abundant in the EFA blend recipe in chapter 3.

Selenium: This trace mineral is essential to immune response and normal functioning of the heart muscle and thyroid gland. There is much evidence to support that selenium helps reduce the risk of cancer, and it's highly recommended for cats with feline leukemia. Rich sources of this substance include wheat germ, fish, garlic, and barley, so if you use the EFA blend from chapter 3 along with green foods, you're adding some very good selenium protection.

The good news is that your pet can get most of the antioxidants it needs from your healthy homemade stews with added EFAs and Anitra's Vita-Mineral Mix. However, I always recommend supplementing with vitamin C and green foods; then your ACES are most definitely covered. Always choose supplements according to your individual pet's needs. Remember that during times of physical or emotional stress, your pet might require more than what you've determined to be its usual maintenance dose. Learn to read your pet and respond accordingly.

> **"My attitude toward tumors is essentially to try and prevent them. Leading scientists have repeatedly found nutritional deficiencies present in cancer patients. Drs. Ewan Cameron and Linus Pauling (the Nobel Prize winner), who have conducted an intense nutritional investigation of cancer, believe that vitamins hold special promise in enhancing resistance and retarding malignancies, 'with ascorbic acid probably possessing the greatest promise of all.'**
>
> **"I feel if an animal is on a good vitamin and mineral program, he is going to have a strong immune system that can neutralize the viruses, chemicals, pollutants, additives, and abnormal cell growth . . . involved in the disease process."**
>
> —WENDELL O. BELFIELD, DVM, author of *How to Have a Healthier Dog*

Let's complete our focus on antioxidants and the immune system builders with the tale of Solo. This former stray had acquired a daunting collection of ailments on the street and was certainly lucky that Ginger had a few aces in the hole.

From Solo to So Healthy

Although Solo was but a pup, he had been through the school of hard knocks. A shameless panhandler, his charm never failed to provide. Luckily for him, one day a bighearted woman took pity, scooped him up, and didn't stop calling her friends until she found a couple who would take him in: Ginger and Gary. At three months old, this big, goofy, black lab mix weighed in at a whopping twenty-five pounds and proved to be a real hooligan. Solo loved chasing squirrels and other varmints from the yard, and although Ginger and Gary hoped he'd grow into a very large and adept watchdog someday, he surprised them with a gentleness that melted their hearts.

Ginger never expected that their new, lively playmate would come fully equipped with a slew of health problems either, so when the vet told them Solo's immune system was severely compromised, it shook them up badly. He found hookworms, tapeworms, and whipworms. Then he pointed out that demodectic mange (caused by a microscopic mite) had caused the excessive hair loss above his eyes. Solo had been constantly peeing around the house, and it turned out that this wasn't a behavioral problem but instead due to a severe urinary tract infection. The vet explained that conventional treatment would normally include an aggressive program of antibiotics and a highly toxic pesticide dip to combat the mange. But he hesitated to treat Solo with chemicals because of how low his immune defenses were and wanted to take a more conservative (and holistic) approach, instead. Solo was a long way from being healthy, and the vet felt the first step was to stabilize him with better food and megadoses of vitamins.

Most people's inclination is to treat symptoms with a pill, but Ginger had learned about the power of vitamins, in conjunction with diet and other naturopathic remedies. So she and Gary breathed a huge sigh of relief when their vet suggested they start with supplements before treating the mange. They agreed on a program of home-

made chicken stew, 5 grams of vitamin C a day (divided into four doses), and three cloves of fresh garlic to help expel worms. The vitamin C was prescribed specifically to boost Solo's immune system, provide antioxidants, and help rid his body of toxins. Ginger even found a soothing topical salve made from beeswax and herbs and decided it couldn't hurt to apply it directly to the infected area around Solo's eyes. The vet anticipated improvement over the course of four to six months and asked Ginger and Gary to report to him biweekly.

Ginger and Gary noticed Solo improving almost immediately. The program of healthy foods and vitamins had a profound effect on his entire body. Within two weeks the tapeworms appeared to be gone. The hair above his eyes began to grow back, and his frequent peeing and straining became a thing of the past. Solo's coat grew so dramatically shiny that Ginger and Gary describe it as an iridescent blue-black. That pathetic street pup had blossomed into a most magnificent creature. Six weeks later, even the vet was amazed. Solo had become the picture of health, and follow-up blood work and tests confirmed that all of his problems had resolved.

Week Six Assessment

❑ Did you add some loving pet massages to your daily rituals this week? Are you noticing and identifying problem areas and body parts that need improvement? Is the massage helping you become consciously aware of the changes that are happening? Are you tuning in to your own natural healing abilities?

❑ Have you started adding vitamin C to your pet's food? What daily dose did you start with and what do you plan to work up to?

❑ How did your pet react to the taste of the vitamin C supplement? Was your pet more receptive when you mixed its vitamin C in with food or a treat? What form of it are you most comfortable using? Do you prefer a liquid or a powder? Did you have to buy some, or were you already using vitamin C in your own diet?

❑ Have you identified any symptoms your pet has that may benefit from supplementing with antioxidants? What conditions do you want to help prevent as your pet grows or ages?

❑ Are there stress-related issues that vitamin C could help?

Daily Play

Remember, playtime every day is mandatory—you owe it to your pet and yourself.

Cat Play Tip: Create a tunnel course. Take four or five brown paper bags from the grocery store and cut a six-inch-wide hole in the bottom of each. Tape them all together end to end (leaving each end open). Now you have a tunnel that's easy to run through and makes a great crinkling sound, and your cat will enjoy playing in it for hours. It may get so excited that it pushes the entire tunnel across the room!

Dog Play Tip: Taking your dog to a dog park is a sure way to get your canine companion running. And the socialization skills it inspires is as important as the exercise. It may be difficult to do this every day, but make time for it on the weekends for sure.

◆ ◆ ◆

This week you began using your ACES—vitamins A, C, and E and the mineral selenium—to fortify your pet's immune system, combat free radicals, and nourish vital body systems. You've experimented with some of my suggestions for working the ACES into your pet's diet; continue to play with this in the remaining two weeks and beyond. Your pet also experienced the soothing, nurturing power of receiving loving massage and should be noticeably calmer and more cheerful as a result. In the coming week, we'll introduce healthy ways to strengthen your pet's structural foundation: its bones, joints, and teeth.

CHAPTER NINE

Week Seven: The Art of Healthy Teeth and Bones

In your journal:

- Complete the Weekly Checkup.

- Schedule your daily play dates.

- Throughout the week, fill in the Week at a Glance.

- At week's end, complete the Weekly Assessment.

This week we get down to great form and focus on healthier teeth and bones. We'll examine the interrelationship between keeping teeth clean and healthy and strengthening the bones. Teeth are alive; they're a part of the skeletal system—so nourishing and protecting one also helps the other. We'll look at the perils of plaque and gum disease, and we'll debunk some of the dental myths that can ambush your pet's health. Because arthritis has become more common in pets than colds, we'll also bone up on supplements and sunlight that can offer our animals the freedom to run, jump, play, and smile brightly their whole lives. You'll learn about the critical role enzymes play in the absorption of vitamins, and delve deeper into how to slow the effects of certain degenerative diseases by focusing on diet, nutrition, and natural health. This chapter gives you much to chew on to help you keep your pet feeling younger.

What to Expect

Clean, bright, white teeth, fresh breath, healthy gums, stronger bones, and a lean, streamlined body ready to run, jump, and play. If your pet was showing signs of aging, you'll notice it starting to look and feel younger again. That enhanced mobility will lift your spirits, so you'll feel better, too!

Real, wholesome, natural food creates a stronger body, including healthy teeth and bones. In fact, holistic vets agree that dogs and cats on healthy, homemade diets have significantly less tartar accumulation and gum disease. They're also less likely to be obese, and this helps with bone and joint problems because unwanted pounds add additional stress to the body's structure and make mobility more difficult. Weight control is important for everybody, but especially important for pets, with tendencies toward musculoskeletal problems.

This chapter covers several specific bone-related ailments, along with my ideas on how best to eliminate or at least alleviate problems and symptoms. Get ready to build on what you learned about vitamins B and C in the last two chapters; this week you'll find out how they also provide for healthy bones and teeth. We'll also cover other natural solutions for hip and joint issues and overall bone health, including the power of sunlight and exercise.

Project: Toss Trashy Tartar Treats

Time to head back to the pantry. If you have food, toys, or chews that promise to decrease tartar, it's time for you to reread the labels and assess their ingredients carefully to see whether the claims have any merit. Any toys and chews that are made outside the United States or that aren't labeled "all natural" may contain chemicals and dyes that can contribute to the degeneration of the teeth. Observe how your pet chews or eats them, particularly if you're in a multiple-pet household. If a pet is prone to hoarding, it may be chewing in a hurry or even swallowing chunks whole to prevent its housemates from getting any.

I have also always been leery about chew sticks or bones basted with flavor enhancers, such as smoked meats; I question how they're preserved. Sure, pets may really like them, but they like chocolate too, and we know how bad that can be for them. (I've heard all too many stories of pets eating chocolate when no one was watching and winding up at the emergency room with near-tragic results.)

Your project this week is to toss any unhealthy chews and in their place introduce safe bones, chicken necks, and healthy crunchies, like hard, raw carrots, as part of a healthy diet and dental hygiene regimen. Within a few weeks, you'll notice marked improvement in your pet's mouth and teeth, and you'll be the primary beneficiary of its fresher breath. These more natural chews also help to create deep levels of emotional canine or feline satisfaction.

For safety's sake, never give your pet any food or chews that can splinter into pieces and become dangerously lodged in the throat or intestinal tract. Dogs love to chew but don't always show the best judgment, so we need to use common sense for them and choose chews (and toys) appropriate for their size and aggressiveness. Get rid of anything that may cause trauma and give your pet a bone—a real, honest-to-goodness bone, healthy, natural, and totally unprocessed, is just the kind of chew nature intends animals to have.

From Bad Breath to Clean Health

Many people are under the misconception that breed dictates mouth health. Although a few breeds, such as bulldogs and Persian cats, have challenges associated with the shape of their mouth or head, in my experience dental problems and gum disease are usually a direct result of the animal being fed poor-quality food. You don't need to spend your pet dollars on kibbles, treats, and chews that promise tartar control or fresh breath. A pet who eats healthfully will smell great, inside and out.

If your pet has bad breath, there are two probable causes: sticky, processed food, which congeals on the teeth, or food stuck in the digestive tract. Highly processed commercial pet foods are difficult for the body to absorb, utilize, or eliminate, so they clog the digestive system, stagnate, and putrefy.

Pets should smell great, and the cleanest-smelling pets are those who eat well. It's not complicated. The basic concepts covered in this book are enough to ensure a clean-smelling pet: always feed real, wholesome, fresh food, and supplement with EFAs, which can unclog the body and help the digestive tract eliminate waste properly. Keep the body clean on the inside, and the outside (teeth and breath) will radiate and reflect the same.

Naturally, your first line of defense is nutrition and supplementation: healthy homemade stew, liver snacks, yogurt, carrots, bones, and supplements containing the B vitamins and extra vitamin C. But yearly dental checkups and cleanings are also important to make sure you're headed down the right path. A good diagnostician can lend deep insights into your pet's health, and at a much deeper level than just the teeth and gums.

Dry Food Does Not Prevent Tooth Decay

Not only is dry food not a good diet, it also doesn't keep teeth clean or prevent tooth decay, even if it says it's specially formulated for teeth or bones. There is no evidence whatsoever that dry food prevents problems in the mouth. That would be like saying if you eat a handful of pretzels each day, your teeth will become healthier and you don't need to brush them. Kibble, like pretzels, clings to the gums, gets stuck between teeth, and causes more tartar buildup, and if you think your pet is getting any chewing exercise at all by eating it, you've simply been fooled by the makers of dry pet food.

What keeps teeth and gums healthy is real foods, like meats, fruits, and vegetables. Enzymes in these unprocessed foods help keep teeth clean. Dry food, with its high gluten content, is probably more likely than any other type of food to cling to teeth and produce bad breath and decay. Raw bones work well to control tartar, as the animal scrapes and gnaws on the rough surfaces from all angles in the mouth. Generally, they like it so much that they'll work on it for hours. And it not only stimulates them physically, it's great for them emotionally— it gives them something important to do.

Choose Your Chew Toys Wisely

Several years ago a variety of greenish-colored chewies came on the market for dogs, and they were met with great enthusiasm. These pressed and shaped bonelike-looking things all boasted healthier ingredients and supposedly freshened the breath. I was given one at a trade show and took it home for Bravo. The components seemed innocent enough: a combination of greens, rice, parsley, and other things like cellulose. Bravo received it with great enthusiasm, jumped on the bed, and began to lick it all over. Within moments, my beautiful white comforter turned bright emerald green, and you can bet treat time ended abruptly!

I remember thinking about all that green dye seeping through my bedding and what sort of chemicals might have been used. That particular brand grew in popularity, but they must have changed the coloring agent because I rarely heard about the messes I first encountered. What I do hear about on a regular basis is that some pets exhibit fairly severe skin or digestive problems when given these kinds of chews, even if they're on a program of healthy food and supplements. Most people don't make the connection that a seemingly innocuous chewie could harm their pet, but we have to condition ourselves to view the whole picture and make better assessments. People usually find that when they quit giving those green chewies to their pet, its skin and digestive problems clear up fairly quickly. So remember, just because something is promoted as "green" doesn't necessarily mean it's good.

Bones Are Nature's Toothbrush

Many holistic practitioners advocate feeding pets raw bones because they're a wonderful source of naturally occurring calcium and phosphorous, both of which are necessary for every aspect of good health. In addition to supporting the teeth nutritionally, bones are really the best way for pets to clean their teeth, and raw, natural bones are often called "nature's toothbrush" (for pets!). Bones are the lazy person's best tool for great pet oral hygiene. And in case you're wondering, raw bones are good for cats, too, especially because cats actually have a higher incidence of tooth decay than dogs.

The best chew toys you can buy are fresh bones from the butcher shop. Look for meaty knuckle bones or soup bones. For under a dollar, you'll have the most effective cleaner for teeth and gums, and the best part is that your pet can attend to its own dental hygiene. This is the way it works in the wild, and I think you'll find that it's vastly preferable to trying to clean your pet's teeth yourself.

For dogs, I suggest one raw bone a week, preferably a thick, beef marrowbone with a little meat on it. Choose a fat knuckle bone or a chunky soup bone from your butcher or the local grocery store. It should be large enough that your dog cannot swallow it. Never feed any pet a cooked chicken or pork bone; these bones are likely to splinter. I've heard about far too many emergency visits to the vet because such bones got lodged in the throat or perforated the stomach.

For cats, I suggest a few vertebrae of a chicken neck, either slightly boiled or raw, once or twice a week. The necks don't splinter because they're made up of more cartilage than bone. If your cats go for them raw, that's great, but I've found that most indoor cats prefer them steamed with a little garlic powder and rosemary added. Beyond making them more palatable, this preparation method also adds beneficial nutrients. You may find that your cat will get a little wild, excited, or primal with the necks. Don't be surprised if they capture the neck and drag the "carcass" away from the rest of the pride to devour.

Since chicken necks come with the whole chicken you've purchased to make your chicken stew, it's like getting a free gift with your purchase. They're generally packaged inside the chicken along with the organs, like the liver and the gizzards. Don't throw anything away. Make use of the whole chicken for all of its goodness and let your cat enjoy the thrill of the neck, like Tabby does.

Tabby: Old-Fashioned Dentistry

Sarah used to think Tabby, her big, striped tomcat, had an odd but adorable habit of chewing his food with his head cocked to one side. The vet, however, viewed it quite differently; he said Tabby had fairly significant gum disease and that thick tartar deposits had accumulated at the back of his mouth. Sarah was quick to defend herself by sharing that she had been feeding Tabby the most expensive dry (but natural) cat food. Because Sarah trusted her holistic vet, she agreed to the gentle teeth scraping he proposed to do without anesthesia. He even showed her that she could relatively easily work in her cat's mouth herself by taking her fingernail and literally plucking the tartar off each tooth, one by one. Gently and gingerly, the two proceeded to scale Tabby's teeth, and in under an hour the job was done. The vet explained that Tabby's mouth had become so sore from the inflammation that he had taken to eating on the side that didn't cause as much pain.

The vet sent Sarah home with a soothing herbal mouth rinse. She was instructed to attend to the scaling at home as needed, and to include raw chicken neck bones as standard procedure. Tabby loved gnawing on the necks and developed his own routine of keeping his teeth clean—the old-fashioned way!

More Diet Boosts for Healthy Teeth

Some holistic practitioners suggest adding a teaspoon of bonemeal to recipes, but I'm not wild about this idea. Bonemeal is a highly processed food that's cooked at extremely high temperatures. As with kibble (or anything) cooked at high temperatures, the valuable nutrients and digestive enzymes the bones may have originally contained could either be cooked out or rendered useless for the body. Even worse, some sources of bonemeal are less than pure; the bones may come from contaminated animals, and they could contain high levels of lead. Although Anitra Frazier used to recommend bonemeal as a source of calcium in her formula, she no longer espouses the benefits and prefers calcium lactate over anything else.

Bones and cartilage—and eggshells—are made of calcium, which is likely the most important nutrient for keeping teeth and bones strong. So once a week I like to grind an organic eggshell into a fine powder (so there are no sharp edges) and feed this to all my pets along with their stew. (I give each animal between 1/2 to 1 teaspoon.) You can do this the old-fashioned way, by using a mortar and pestle, or use a food processor. Pets can also get extra calcium from fresh, raw bones, yogurt, and green leafy vegetables.

Carrots, rich in beta-carotene, are another great way to promote healthy teeth and slip vitamin A into the diet naturally—whether you feed them raw, grate them over a snack, or toss them into a stew. Try giving your canine friend a raw carrot. Not all dogs like them, but if you're lucky enough to have a dog who does, there's no better snack stick for it to chew on. Liver, eggs, and unsalted peanut butter provide folate (the natural form of folic acid) as well as vitamin A, and all are tasty treats that will enhance and brighten your pet's smile.

Also keep in mind that B complex and vitamin C are important for strong teeth and bones. Whether for prevention or to alleviate an existing condition, it's easy to supplement either. For B complex, give your pet a teaspoon of nutritional yeast or an appropriate amount of Anitra's Vita-Mineral Mix (see chapter 7). Refer back to chapter 8 for recommendations on vitamin C supplements and doses.

Do-It-Yourself Inspections and Remedies

The body responds quickly to the effects of healthy food, but some amount of tartar is, unfortunately, a fact of life where teeth are concerned, whether you're a dog, cat, or human. Tartar can lead to inflamed and infected gums and periodontal diseases, so it's important you check the teeth and gums of your pet regularly. If you're not sure what to look for, consult your holistic vet. Basically, teeth should be white and gums pink, although not all breeds have pink gums. Get to know the inside of your pet's mouth intimately, the same way you've gotten to know the rest of its body. You should perform oral inspections on a regular basis (at least once a month) to see if there are any abscesses, loose teeth, swollen gums, or other irregularities. A red line close to the teeth along the gum line should sound an alarm that there may be an underlying health problem to address.

If your pet is uncomfortable with you exploring its mouth, you'll need to work to get it accustomed to your monthly inspections. One of the best ways to do this is to sit down in a comfortable position and stroke your pet's face lovingly while saying, with a kind, soft voice, that you're just making sure it is healthy. Stroke over your pet's eyes, forehead, and ears, and run your hands over all sides of its mouth and muzzle. Pay particular attention to the muzzle area and begin to rub gently with a circular motion. After a few minutes, move your fingers over the lips and pull them up past the teeth to examine the gums. You can gently massage the gums while you're doing this procedure. As your pet becomes more accustomed to being touched in the mouth and you become more adept at the procedure, any stress associated with your monthly checkups will disappear. Most pets actually enjoy being touched and caressed in the mouth, just as they enjoy it on other parts of their bodies.

Make sure you take a good look. Obviously, anything red, inflamed, or bleeding is not good. But be aware that there are other, less obvious signs of dental problems, as Tabby's story showed, such as drooling, chewing on one side of the mouth, turning the head while chewing, irritability, or dropping food because it's too painful to chew. Many typical misbehaviors may also be indicative of periodontal disease, so instead of sentencing your pet to the doghouse, consider throwing it a bone!

Though attending to your pet's dental health probably won't be your favorite aspect of dealing with your furry friend, motivate yourself by keeping in mind that your pet will be happier and healthier with your regular checkups and their own form of natural dental hygiene. If you discover any major problems during your checkups, you'll need to consult your vet. But you may be able to treat minor problems at home using simple remedies you can make yourself. All of the remedies below are safe and effective for you to use, as well. I encourage you to always try the products you choose on yourself before you use them on your pet. You create a higher level of awareness when you put yourself in your pet's position. When you experience first "paw" how everything feels, tastes, or smells, you'll make wiser choices.

Anitra Frazier's Healthy Mouth Formula: This formula is great for basic hygiene and regular mouth maintenance. It is especially useful after the teeth have been scaled and tartar is removed. This formula can also be used to soothe and reduce swelling of the gums. Mix together $^1/_4$ cup springwater or distilled water, $^1/_8$ teaspoon salt, and 3 drops of tincture of myrrh. Apply to the gums once daily with cotton swabs if a problem exists, or once a week for prevention.

Calendula: If your pet has been in an accident in which teeth were broken or knocked out, you can give it immediate relief by applying the soothing herb calendula directly to the gums. It helps stop bleeding, promotes rapid healing, and eases the pain. Purchase calendula in a tincture or extract form. It's available in most well-stocked health food stores. Mix 10 drops in 1 cup of warm water. Apply gently to the affected area using a soaked gauze pad as a compress.

Flushing Mouthwash: Dilute 10 drops of calendula tincture and $^1/_4$ teaspoon sea salt in 1 cup of warm water. You can use it as a flushing mouthwash, applied with an eyedropper, once or twice monthly. If your pet has an infected area in its mouth, (punctures, swelling, or irritation), soak a small gauze pad in the solution and gently apply it directly to the problem area. Continue flushing for 2 to 3 minutes, once or twice daily.

Voyko's Fresh Breath Rinse: Pour 1 cup of boiling water over a fresh mint sprig or peppermint tea bag. Cover, cool to room temperature, and let sit overnight. Use cotton swab or your finger to rub the mint tea on your pet's teeth, gums, and tongue. This tea is also excellent for digestion.

Joint and Bone Conditions and Solutions

There are several factors to blame for the distressing increase in pet joint and bone problems. Poor diet and lack of exercise are probably by far the greatest contributors. Inbreeding is often blamed for the congenital predisposition to specific ailments. While this may be true, many of the symptoms can be prevented or alleviated by using the whole pet approach.

ARTHRITIS AND HIP DYSPLASIA

Although we think of arthritis as a problem among senior pets, this may not always be the case. As of this writing, arthritis is said to affect one in five dogs over the age of seven, so it's no wonder that hip and joint supplements pack the shelves of pet aisles and pet stores. An ounce of prevention is, of course, worth many pounds of cure, and diet and nutrition can play a huge role in proper development of the musculoskeletal system. Beyond that, supplementation is important and can help at all ages and stages. But don't underestimate the strain an overly fat body can have on an animal's joints and bones, which brings us back to the basics—a nutritionally balanced diet.

Some signs of degenerative skeletal problems are painful, stiff joints that make walking or rising a problem. A pet in pain may have difficulty with or completely avoid jumping or climbing stairs. Some even display increased nervousness, depression, or aggression. Pay close attention to what your pet is telling you. It's important to read your pet's body language to understand it from a whole pet perspective.

Hip dysplasia occurs mostly in larger breeds of dogs or dogs with longer bodies and shorter legs, like dachshunds and basset hounds. Only recently has this problem been studied in cats, and it turns out that just as in dogs larger, heavier breeds like Persians and Maine coon cats may be more prone to developing it.

Two nutraceuticals are enormously beneficial in combating hip dysplasia and arthritis: glucosamine and chondroitin. (*Nutraceuticals*—also called *functional foods*—are natural, bioactive foods or food-derived substances with health-promoting, disease-preventing, or medicinal properties.) These supplements are immensely popular for people with joint pain, and more recently they've increased in popularity in veterinary circles because of the immediate benefits they seem to produce in all animals. Personally, I've witnessed and read many reports of their effectiveness in eliminating stiffness and promoting greater mobility in both dogs and cats. I'll explain these supplements in greater detail below, under "Reduce Inflammation, Increase Absorption."

ENZYMES, DIGESTION, AND BONE HEALTH

Enzymes are specialized proteins found in all living things that control every chemical process in the body. They act as catalysts, facilitating biochemical reactions. For example, when calcium is incorporated into bone, enzymes help make it happen. Enzymes also play a key role in digestion of food and absorption of nutrients. Live enzymes naturally occur in foods, helping them to ripen and even decay. They're often destroyed during refrigeration and cooking, and they're totally destroyed by microwaving. Irradiated vegetables and fruits may appear to remain fresher longer, but they're devoid of live enzymes. Fruits and vegetables flash-frozen at peak ripeness contain more enzymes than fresh vegetables that have been refrigerated.

When we destroy enzymes in foods, it's harder for the body to utilize the food's nutrients, and the situation with supplements is similar. If vitamins and other supplements aren't combined with live enzymes, they tend to pass right through the system. You may be wasting your money on vitamins if they're used in the absence of enzymes. One solution is to combine supplements with nutritious, enzyme-rich foods to help the body process them more efficiently.

Coenzyme Q10, sometimes referred to as CoQ10 or vitamin Q10, is an antioxidant found in every cell in the body. It helps control the flow of oxygen and better enables the body to produce energy from food. Many holistic practitioners use it to treat pets with periodontal problems and heart disease, and it has also been recommended for overweight and underweight dogs and cats with immune problems, decreased physical capacity, and diabetes. Some vets use it as a complementary adjunct to dental cleaning, and they suggest giving CoQ10 in pill form or diluting it in water and rubbing it directly on the gums.

There have been several studies supporting the efficacy of CoQ10. Its use makes sense to me because I believe that obesity, dental problems, bone health, and arthritis are all related to an inability to break food down, which leads us back to proper digestion and enzymes.

The popularity of CoQ10 is ever-increasing and there are many distributors of this highly desirable nutraceutical. CoQ10 from Japan is usually made using natural methods, but in recent years, it has become more difficult to procure. The Chinese have started making CoQ10 as well, but my understanding is that their version is generally synthetic and purportedly not as effective as the natural version. Whenever possible, opt for Japanese or natural-source CoQ10.

REDUCE INFLAMMATION, INCREASE ABSORPTION

Enzymes can help reduce inflammation, prevent harmful blood clotting, and support the immune system. These properties make enzymes critical for pets with bruises, sprains, swelling, edema, injuries, arthritis, hip dysplasia, and pain of any kind. Because enzymes assist all biochemical reactions in the body, it's easy to understand their importance in digestion, and healing of soft tissues, but you may wonder what relevance they have to seemingly static structures, like teeth and bones.

To understand the connection, let's take a closer look at glucosamine and chondroitin, mentioned above as important aids for arthritis and hip dysplasia. The reason these two naturally occurring substances are so often combined is because of their complementary functions: glucosamine directly builds collagen, the foundation and pliable supportive substance in cartilage, and chondroitin protects cartilage from breaking down and ensures that the joints have enough fluid to provide optimum mobility and flexibility. In short, the combination provides for both rebuilding and maintenance of joints. But their combined effectiveness is significantly enhanced when they're used holistically, blended with enzymes for palatability and absorption and with vitamin C, which is so important for collagen.

In my company's developmental research for a glucosamine and chondroitin supplement, we use a powdered form of each and combine them with apple pectin and beet powder, two great sources of live enzymes. Pets love the taste of the apple pectin, and both of these healthy foods help the body absorb and retain these important nutraceuticals. If glucosamine and chondroitin are supplemented without additional enzymes, the body tends to pass them out of the system very quickly, and you wind up purchasing a product that becomes little more than very expensive urine. Needless to say, the therapeutic effects of such products are only a fraction of what they could be.

Although there are double-blind, scientific studies supporting the combination of enzymes with glucosamine and chondroitin, there's no better testament to reduced swelling and pain-free movement than an old dog performing new tricks with the help of this powerful blend of supplements. The combination helps lubricate joints and vertebrae and promotes healthy cartilage, ligaments, and tendons. Conventional and holistic vets alike recommend regular supplementation of glucosamine and chondroitin, not only for pets with arthritis and hip dysplasia, but as a preventative measure against future problems, especially for pets with tendencies toward known weaknesses, like overweight pets or breeds that are overly large, short-legged, or long-backed.

Crumpet: A City Dog Gone Country

Even as a puppy, Crumpet was generally sedentary and slow-moving. This lumbering English bulldog lived in the lap of luxury and had everything a respectable New York City girl should have: jeweled collars, an overstuffed wrought iron bed, and handmade bowls with her name inscribed on them. Her family, Karen and Roy, had given her everything but the one thing she seemed to want most, a canine companion to play with.

By the time Karen had found the house of her dreams, a Victorian mansion in the country, Crumpet was nine years old. Seemingly late in Crumpet's life, they finally got her a little brother to help motivate her to run and play on the property, hoping to spark some new life in her. But all too soon the painful truth became clear: Crumpet's joints hurt way too much for her to take advantage of the liveliness of her new playmate. She was large for her breed (about sixty-five pounds) and had a long back and short legs, so she was unfortunately predisposed to developing joint problems. It made Karen sad to think that her dream of the frolicking pair might never come true.

Crumpet had been used to sleeping in Karen and Roy's bedroom at the old apartment (a one-floor flat), but try as she might, she couldn't make her way up the steep flight of stairs in the new house. Karen resigned herself to Crumpet's dilemma, but then she heard about my success with aging pets and tracked me down. Since Karen was so busy with renovations and didn't want to take the time to make her own supplements, I suggested that she try my company's hip and joint supplement with glucosamine, chondroitin, apple pectin, and kelp. "Just sprinkle it over the food," I told her. "To Crumpet, it will taste like candy!"

Karen picked up my Hip, Hip, Hooray formula at the health food store and started using it right away. Within days, she reported that Crumpet was literally bounding through the property with her little brother Morsel in tow. It took a few more weeks, but best of all was that she was finally sleeping soundly in her beautiful wrought iron bed in the room at the top of the stairs.

Tips on Easing Arthritis Pain

There are many simple solutions to help relieve or eliminate the aches and pains your pet suffers due to arthritis. Here are just a few:

- Feed a healthy, wholesome diet and ensure your pet is not overweight.

- Vitamin C relieves pain and inflammation, detoxifies the body, and builds collagen. I've seen cats and dogs crippled with arthritis become active again after taking megadoses of vitamin C.

- Provide other supplements that reduce swelling, build collagen, and lubricate and support bones, ligaments, and joints (glucosamine, chondroitin, Anitra's Vita-Mineral Mix, and EFAs).

- Provide steps or ramps and raise water and food bowls to assist your pet until its body strengthens and greater mobility returns.

Sunshine, Exercise, and Strong Bones: The Vitamin D and Calcium Connection

Don't let the sun go down on another day without a brisk walk, an off-leash run, a good chase, or a refreshing swim. Most of us know that any type of weight-bearing exercise helps build strong bone and muscle. But do you know that a day without sunshine is like a day without vitamin D? Sunshine increases the body's natural production of vitamin D, which in turn allows the body to absorb more calcium. Calcium is crucial for strong bones, so in addition to working on your pet's diet, be sure it gets plenty of outdoor, daylight exercise.

A good friend of mine with several pets keeps a beautiful garden in a large, fenced yard. She lets her dogs and cat run loose while she rakes, pulls weeds, and tills the soil. If her pets can't find something to chase or chew on their own, she'll toss a stick or pinecone. Her cats love it when she tickles them with a vine and coaxes them to chase it. Gardening, stretching, and all that great exercise not only helps keep her own osteoporosis at bay, it stimulates her pets, gets them to move, and gives them a healthy dose of sunlight to strengthen their bones.

If possible, and if you can provide a safe outdoor environment, make sure all of your pets have access to sunlight and exercise in some form or another. This is especially important for senior dogs and cats, who tend to become sedentary if you don't get them up and moving. If your cat doesn't have access to the great outdoors, it's really important to create a comfortable window perch on the sunniest side of your home. For cats without access to a safe form of sunshine, it's especially important to add cod liver oil to the diet. This great oil not only supplies EFAs, but also provides vitamin D, which acts as a potent sunshine substitute.

The interconnection between sunlight, vitamin D, calcium, and exercise for your pet's bone and joint health is a great illustration of why the whole pet approach makes such perfect sense. As it turns out, sunlight and time outdoors are critical for optimum nutrition, allowing the body to make and utilize nutrients more effectively. So conscious choices about play dates actually enhance your pet, both emotionally and physically!

- Line favorite napping spots with soft, cushy pillows and blankets. Add a moist, warm towel if the pain is persistent.

- Give frequent, gentle, loving massages.

- Ensure that your pet gets gentle exercise. Frequent, short play periods are better than longer play dates, which may place undue stress on the body and the muscles.

- Try some of the newer beds on the market that have safe heating systems built right into them.

Week Seven Assessment

❑ What treats, chews, and other products have you identified that claimed to help your pet's teeth, breath, and the like? Given everything you've learned in this book, are there chemicals and other ingredients in these products that you're suspicious of?

❑ Did you thoroughly examine your pet's mouth, teeth, and gums? Did you have to prepare yourself mentally to explore its mouth thoroughly? Are you getting the hang of it?

❑ Have you offered your pet its own toothbrush? (Raw bones, of course!) What kind of bones did you get? Was it eager to get down to business and brush its teeth? How did your pet respond to its new bones? Did the bones bring out the primal beast in your furry friend? Make note of how fast the bones work to help remedy the tartar buildup.

❑ Did you take some time to make and use any of the healthy mouth remedies? Did you try them yourself? How did they feel?

❑ Are you hoping to correct any existing musculoskeletal problems? Do you have a growing pet and a goal of helping prevent problems? Or you are consciously trying to support an older pet in its aging process? Is your pet moving slower, more gingerly, favoring a foot, or sitting sideways? Does it seem stiff and hesitant to do things, like running, jumping, or climbing? When did you begin to notice those changes?

Daily Play

This week you learned another reason to make time to play with your pet in the great outdoors (safely, of course): the sun is a great asset to a holistic pet, providing free vitamin D and enhancing calcium absorption—so use it!

Cat Play Tip: Make your kitty jump through hoops—in a good way! Start with a hula hoop close to the ground and get your cat to walk through it. If need be, lure them with a fresh treat. Once it gets the idea, raise the hoop a little more each week until you reach a challenging but not impossible level. The standard for professional competitive agility trials is two feet.

Dog Play Tip: Don't overlook the oldest dog-and-human game of them all: fetching a stick or a ball. My dog Jasmine loves it and will play for hours. Playing catch and fetch helps keep dogs young and limber. It also gets you outdoors, so your dog will benefit from the sun and fresh air, as well.

◆ ◆ ◆

This week we put the spring back into your pet's step, strengthened its teeth, and supplemented with nutraceuticals and enzymes, along with a splash of the sun. We've banished any vestiges of nasty doggie or kitty breath, and your pet is feeling fabulous!

With just one week to go in the eight-week plan, we've covered nearly every aspect of what your pet needs for vibrant health and contentment. These last seven weeks have been packed with learning and changes. I know that, by now, your pet is feeling as good about the whole pet way of life as you are. So let's take the final step and move to the outside of the body. I've got a glorious day in store for both of you, and you've definitely earned it! Read on.

CHAPTER TEN

Week Eight:
The Art of the Spa

In your journal:

- Complete the Weekly Checkup.

- Schedule your daily play dates.

- Throughout the week, fill in the Week at a Glance.

- At week's end, complete the Weekly Assessment and take your final Whole Pet Portrait.

This week we're going to lavish your pet with the loving art of grooming and create a whole pet spa designed to nurture both you and your pet with healing baths, soothing combs and brushes, and gentle ear and eye treatments. Stimulate the senses, both yours and your pet's, as you begin to familiarize yourself with aromatic botanicals and herbs. After seven weeks of delicious food, wholesome treats, and healthy supplements, including EFAs, your fluffy angel is already glowing. The finishing touches you'll learn this week will help brighten your pet's natural beauty and keep it parasite-free.

You'll learn about a few excellent grooming techniques and some must-have products that you can purchase at the health food store. I'll also share some simple solutions for common pet problems and remedies you can easily make at home. Of course, I'd never use or recommend chemical products, so this chapter's holistic home spa provides a chemical-free head-to-tail treatment liberally filled with safety, tranquility, and enlightenment. This healthy, cleansing ritual nurtures our animals and the environment that we all live in together. The simple practice of grooming, approached mindfully, strengthens your bonds with your beloved companion. It will be a pleasurable experience that reduces stress, improves health, and integrates body, mind, and spirit.

What to Expect

Lots of love and attention for your pet, and lots of love and appreciation from your pet. I truly believe this transfer of positive energies creates a harmony in our world; as we give, we surely receive. Relax and enjoy as you experience the healing power of touch and smell.

Project: Grooming Cabinet Makeover

Get out your magnifying glass. It's time to read the fine print and see what's really in the shampoos, flea treatments, ear ointments, and other grooming aids you've been using. Ferret out all of these products from wherever you may have them stashed and toss out all questionable products that contain artificial fragrances or chemical coloring agents and dyes. A good rule of thumb is that if you can't identify or even pronounce the ingredients in a product, you should toss it out. I'll give you more detailed information on what to toss and safe alternatives later in the chapter, but to help you get started on your project, here's a list of ingredients to avoid: propylene glycol, sodium laurel sulfate, sodium laureth sulfate, petroleum, DEET, diazinon, carbaryl, piperonyl butoxide, fenthion, cythioate, mineral oil, isopropyl alcohol, and fragrances. (For a more complete list, see the third edition of *Dr. Pitcairn's Complete Guide to Natural Health for Dogs and Cats*). "Fragrance" may seem like a benign ingredient, but be aware that a single synthetic fragrance can contain hundreds of chemicals to produce a particular scent, and many are derived from petroleum.

Learning to Read between the Lines

As you work through this chapter, we'll replace conventional products laced with chemicals with gentler, healthier options. We'll look at each category or product type and learn about ingredients that are unnecessary and could actually be harmful to you or your pet. The goal is to cleanse and revitalize using only healthy products, so we'll also look at how to shop for the best spa solutions, including nature's apothecary— real herbs. As a first step, let's take a look at which types of products and ingredients are dangerous, which are misleading, and which are 100 percent pure and natural.

IF IT ISN'T SAFE FOR YOU, IT ISN'T SAFE FOR YOUR PET!

Toxic chemicals have long been prevalent in the pet products industry. Far too may dips, sprays, and collars bear warnings like these:

- Wash hands thoroughly after use.

- Do not breathe fumes.

- Wear rubber gloves.

- And the one that scares me the most: May be harmful to fish and wildlife!

These labels aren't general warnings or cautions; they're needed advice because the products contain toxic and dangerous materials. Even worse, many of these chemicals are applied to our pets and left on indefinitely. Remember, the skin is the body's largest organ, and it's permeable, so anything used topically on the skin is absorbed into the bloodstream. Help your pet's skin do its job of protecting your pet from environmental pollutants by not intentionally applying harmful chemicals to your pet's skin or coat, such as shampoos containing flea repellents. Anything toxic that comes in contact with your pet (including pesticides and fertilizers) can wreak havoc and attack its immune system. It's no wonder that some pets have seizures or seem drugged, nervous, and lethargic after a flea bath or a monthly spot-on treatment for parasite control. Whether you groom your pet yourself or rely on a professional, it's important to replace conventional products with healthier, more natural options. Most of the people I know insist on bringing their own safe and natural products to the groomers, and they make sure their wishes are followed. Unless you're sure your groomer is like-minded, it's better to be safe than sorry.

Become accustomed to questioning everything on product labels, and don't ever hesitate to call the manufacturer and get explanations as to why they've chosen any ingredients they use. Make them accountable for their products. A good and reputable company will know how their products work and why they've chosen to use all of their ingredients. Never be shy about educating yourself when it comes to the health of your pet. Conscientious, caring pet owners call me every day for answers to their questions.

THE (NOT REALLY) NATURAL PRODUCTS

As with selecting holistic food or treats, it's important to read between the lines when you decipher the labels of grooming products. Don't be distracted by clever, flowered designs on bottles and "green" packaging. Many companies try to fool the public with wholesome and natural images. I've seen shampoos claiming to be totally botanical, with pretty floral graphics and butterflies and the words "herbal" or "organic" on the label that proved to be anything but wholesome. A closer inspection of such products may indicate that they contain chemically compounded fragrances that may smell natural but are actually synthetic. Many topical salves and ointments claiming to be herbal are petroleum based. Even the "organic" conundrum runs rampant in grooming products, allowing manufacturers to bring to market non-organic products as organic. As I've mentioned before, there is little government regulation when it comes to pet products; the pet industry has been mostly self-regulated throughout its history. Topical products, with the exception of pesticides, are almost never scrutinized. It's important to read labels carefully and take the time to educate yourself so you can ensure that your pet is getting what you really want it to have: pure, unadulterated, natural products without antagonistic elements that may interfere with its immune system, recovery, or wellness.

Truly Natural Ingredients

Natural ingredients are those derived from a living organism or something found naturally in nature and that haven't been chemically processed. Most vitamins, minerals, and essential oils are considered natural products as long as they aren't synthesized or chemically extracted or processed.

The term *botanical* means "relating to plants," and botanicals are products derived from plant material. Herbs and flowers valued for their medicinal, flavorful, and aromatic qualities are also botanicals and are listed individually as ingredients in natural products.

SOME HERBS COMMONLY USED FOR GROOMING

The following glossary describes some of the herbs and extracts most frequently used in many body care products, for humans and animals alike. There are many other beneficial herbs not listed here that may also be valuable to your pet's overall health. But before you use or grow any herbs yourself, become familiar with their specific applications, limitations, and warnings.

Almond Oil: Sweet almond oil is rich in essential fatty acids and vitamins A and E. Because it penetrates so well, it's great for softening and conditioning dry and inflamed skin, paw pads, and noses. Since it's very thick and greasy, it shouldn't be applied to a pet's hair or coat.

Aloe Vera: Known as the secret to Cleopatra's beauty, the fresh sap from this medicinal plant is used in many soothing and healing moisturizing creams. It's rich in vitamins A, C, and E, has antibacterial, antiviral, and anti-inflammatory properties, and penetrates well as it cleanses, moisturizes, and eases pain. It's wonderful for helping soothe chapped skin, dermatitis, eczema, and burns. People love to grow it in their homes, and one reason is because the leaves may be broken and the sap applied directly to skin.

Calendula: This rejuvenating, colorful, and powerful herb has long been valued for its extraordinary healing and anti-inflammatory properties. Calming and antiseptic, it's used to cleanse, soothe, and heal hot spots, cracked skin, rashes, burns, insect bites, and chapped areas. It's my favorite topical herb.

Cedarwood: This woody, sweet-smelling sedative is used as an antiseptic and insect repellent, but it must be used in a diluted form to avoid irritating the skin. This multifaceted herb can be used as a soothing addition to a natural shampoo or flea spray, and in a highly diluted form, it's helpful in eliminating dandruff. The aroma has calming properties that can soothe the nervous system.

Chamomile: Egyptians dedicated this sweet, apple-scented herb to the sun and worshipped it for its ability to calm and soothe the body, mind, and soul. Best known as a tea, it's found on many a grocery store shelf, but its anti-inflammatory aspects make it useful for healing sensitive skin and mucus membranes.

Citronella: A tall aromatic grass from southern Asia produces citronella oil, with its rich, distinctive scent. Citronella oil repels biting insects like mosquitoes, fleas, and ticks, and it's commonly used in a wide variety of products for that purpose, from candles to lotions and sprays to shampoos. Highly concentrated, it must be used in a diluted form to prevent skin irritation.

Clove: Warm, highly aromatic, and soothing to the senses, clove has long been used in dentistry to deaden pain. In diluted form, it appears in herbal grooming aids because of its anesthetic, antibacterial, and antifungal qualities, as well as its ability to help repel certain insects.

Comfrey: This herb's name is derived from the Latin word *conferta*, which means "grow together," and since at least 400 B.C.E., this healing herb has been used to treat wounds, stop bleeding, and even mend broken bones. It's used externally to support tissue regeneration and is found in many herbal conditioners and healing salves for a variety of skin problems.

Eucalyptus: This stimulating and distinct aromatic herb is well known for its ability to repel many different kinds of insects. In a diluted form, it's used in many pet shampoos as an antiseptic and flea repellent. This oil is very strong and can irritate the eyes, nose, and genitals. It should never be applied full strength to the skin.

Eyebright: Also known as euphrasia, eyebright has been used by Greek herbalists for over two thousand years to treat eye problems, including inflammation, discharge. swelling, and eyestrain. Its anti-inflammatory and astringent properties make it useful for relieving runny, sore, itchy eyes caused by colds or allergies. For pets, this herb must only be used in a highly diluted form in a saline solution (see Anitra's Herbal Eyewash recipe on page 213).

Goldenseal: This medicinal plant gets its name from its bright yellow roots. Native Americans used this natural antibiotic as an astringent to treat skin irritations, wounds, and sore, inflamed eyes. Goldenseal is recommended by naturalists and homeopaths as an ingredient in eye-wash and mouthwash, and in the treatment of skin problems, but it should never be used full strength and must be highly diluted for pets (see Anitra's Herbal Eyewash recipe on page 213).

Horehound: Ancient Greeks used this menthol-like herb to treat wounds, and the Egyptians used it to repel flies. Today it's known for its antiseptic and antibacterial qualities and is used in a diluted form to cleanse and soothe skin infections and abrasions.

Jojoba: This therapeutic ingredient was first used by Native Americans to treat sores and wounds. These days, it's commonly found in many pet and human shampoos, as well as healing balms. It does wonders for dry, flaky skin and helps restore elasticity and suppleness.

Lavender: Derived from Latin, *lavender* literally means "to wash." This herb's fresh, clean scent and soothing antiseptic properties have made it the most widely used herb, especially in bath and massage products. It helps calm nerves and ease tension, and may be added to any herbal grooming aid (in a diluted form) or used in a sachet for a lovely aromatic effect.

Pennyroyal: A member of the mint family, this natural enemy of fleas has a powerful effect in eliminating and repelling most pests, a quality that's long been known, as its name is derived from the Latin word *pulex*, which means "flea." This is a medicinal herb and should only be used externally in a highly diluted form in shampoos, sprays, or other grooming aids.

Peppermint: Prized for its medicinal benefits, this invigorating, antiseptic pain reliever is used in many topical products to soothe skin irritations. It's both relaxing and stimulating, and it increases blood flow. The aroma helps relieve tension and its cool, soothing sensation eases muscle pain. It must be used in a diluted form to prevent skin irritations on pets.

Pine Needle: Fresh-smelling and invigorating, this herb has been used in saunas and steam baths for centuries to ease sore muscles and arthritic pain, as well as strengthen the system. It moisturizes and sterilizes, so it's excellent for healing wounds, repairing damaged skin, and clearing blocked pores. It's also an excellent flea repellent but must be used in a diluted form to prevent skin irritations on pets.

Rosemary: Considered sacred in many countries, rosemary is recommended in the treatment of sores, bruises, and wounds. Its piney fragrance aids in its use as a liniment on sore muscles. Rosemary is most commonly used as a preservative in many topical products, but it's also known to help repel ticks and fleas and acts as an invigorating hair tonic.

Sage: An old favorite for controlling dandruff, sage has long been used to strengthen and energize hair. It's wonderful for the skin, especially the paws. A soothing, antiseptic tonic, its fragrant aroma is cleansing and purifying for both mind and body. Sage has been used as an insect repellent, but it must be used in a diluted form to prevent skin irritations on pets.

Southernwood: This herb's lemony aroma is effective against insects, intestinal worms, and some bacteria. The leaves may be added to a bath to invigorate the body, and it's known for helping to fight bacteria and blemishes on the skin.

St. John's Wort: This mighty herb is wonderfully calming and soothing, helps eliminate pain, and is said to repair nerve tissue after trauma. Herbalists credit it with creating a sense of wellness and use it as a topical dressing on wounds of all kinds.

Tea Tree Oil: This powerful antiseptic and fungicide from an Australian plant heals skin infections and wounds. It's highly disinfecting without being toxic and supports the body as it battles such topical problems as insect bites, fungal infections, wounds, and abrasions. A magnificent cleanser, it's found in better pet shampoos, flea sprays, and healing salves.

There are so many herbs, oils, and extracts that are beneficial for you and your pet that there's no way I could describe them all here. But there are many great books devoted to this subject, and I urge you to continue to explore the realm of possibilities. Buy a book on herbs and keep it handy. I love reading about the many uses of herbs, grow some of my own, and continue to learn more about them all the time.

Now let's take a look at specific categories of products. I'll help you understand what to toss, what to look for, and why.

Shampoo

You want a shampoo that's detergent free, biodegradable, hypoallergenic, and free of artificial colors, fragrances, and preservatives. There are many such products on the market, and you'll find exactly what you need, including safe shampoos with pest control properties or conditioning elements; just be ready to read the ingredient panels.

TOSS OUT

Get rid of any shampoos containing sodium laurel sulfate, sodium laureth sulfate, or ammonium laurel sulfate. These are the most common foaming ingredients in personal care products for both humans and pets. These inexpensive and caustic detergents lather well but are typically difficult to rinse out, especially for pets with longer hair. In fact, they can double the time required for the whole grooming process Most people assume thick, rich foam is beneficial for the skin and coat, but in reality these chemical additives actually dry the skin and may even promote hair loss. Even worse, sodium laurel sulfate reacts with other commonly used ingredients to form potentially carcinogenic nitrates and dioxins. Large amounts of nitrates may enter the blood from just one shampooing and can cause long-term problems, especially in the sensitive eye, nose, and ear areas.

Don't be fooled by coconut-based shampoos either. Saponified coconut oil is indeed a good thing, but coconut-based products usually just use lauric acid, which is chemically extracted from coconut husks and combined with sodium or ammonia. Coconut-based products can remove the protective lipid coatings from the coat and skin. I don't recommend oatmeal baths either, as they clog up the pores, and despite oatmeal's reputation for being soothing to the skin, I have found it to create many kinds of skin irritations and even outbreaks of pimples or blisters. Lanolin, a product derived from sheep's wool, may seem safe enough, but it can coat hair follicles and attract dirt and dust, making it necessary to bathe your pet more often.

LOOK FOR

I highly recommend pure, simple, castile shampoos with saponified oils of coconut, jojoba, olive, and rosemary. Castile is basically an entirely vegetable-based soap, whereas many other soaps are made from animal fat (tallow). This environmentally sound soap was named for the Castile region of Spain, where it was originally made with the local olive oil.

Saponification is the process of turning pure oil into soap. Heating the oil and mixing it with lye yields a pure, mild substance that quickly and efficiently rinses out of all types of coats. Despite lye's reputation as being harsh, when used to make soap there is no gentler formulation on the planet. All you need to do is add water, and voilà! You get

How Often Should Cats and Dogs Get a Bath?

Most cats never need a bath, especially if they're on a healthy food and vitamin regimen. However, cats love to be clean, and most long-haired cats do need professional grooming from time to time to keep their coat healthy. Whether short- or long-haired, any cat should be lovingly bathed if it's experiencing a major flea problem or if it's soiled itself accidentally. If it should be necessary to bathe your cat, remember, even though your kitty may be reluctant, it should still be a pleasurable experience for all involved. If your cat has a perpetually greasy tail or a coat problem, a bath is not the answer. This is definitely a signal that something else is wrong and that an immediate change in diet is crucial to its well-being.

If your dog is on a wholesome, natural diet, it shouldn't need a bath more than once every two months or so. Try not to bathe your dog too often (unless your dog has gotten into something really unpleasant), as this can strip important natural oils out of the coat and skin and leave your dog much more susceptible to fleas and ticks. Even after a romp in the ocean, I just rinse the sand off my dogs with plain water. I've found that any remaining salt water is healing for their skin and actually acts as a natural coat conditioner, too.

a rich, foamy, emollient lather that cleans better than anything else I know of and rinses out easily. I find that saponified oils in a shampoo base can cut my own grooming time in half. I particularly like olive oil for its smooth, creamy, moisturizing lather, and coconut because it's rich in glycerin, which hydrates the skin.

When working with basic castile soaps to create an effective shampoo, try adding a small amount of essential oils (found at health food stores) to fill your home with lovely natural fragrances that enrich the soul. I prefer the fresh, clean aromas of peppermint, eucalyptus, or sage, as they also help repel all kinds of insects. You only need to add a small amount of essential oil: $1/8$ teaspoon of either peppermint, eucalyptus, or sage oil is sufficient for 16 ounces of liquid castile soap. Your pet will smell delicious, and the aroma will linger on your dog or cat's skin for several days.

Conditioners

After a recent browsing through the grooming section of my local pet store for rinse-out or leave-in coat conditioners, I came to the conclusion that it's safer and certainly more cost-effective to make conditioners myself. Some pets have thick, coarse coats or even double coats like Sweetie, my Hungarian kuvasz. It's easy to groom her after a bath using brushes or combs to apply conditioner. Jasmine, my Australian shepherd, has a slick coat that needs very little attention after a bath. Decide if conditioner is appropriate for your dog or cat based on the length of its coat and its general condition overall.

TOSS OUT

Get rid of any products with the petroleum derivatives propylene glycol, mineral oil, and isopropyl alcohol; all are petroleum derivatives and are found in many human cosmetic products, as well, including foundation, cleansers, and moisturizers. Propylene glycol carries moisture and makes products feel very slick, fooling you into thinking it's helpful for conditioning the coat. Research has linked propylene glycol to liver and kidney damage, and it's very harmful if swallowed. Mineral oil locks chemicals against the skin, which could, in fact, block pores and prevent the skin from breathing properly, and isopropyl alcohol actually dries and cracks the skin.

LOOK FOR

Conditioners need not be complex formulations; all-natural herbs and oils will often do the trick. I suggest Anitra's Rosemary Conditioner, a simple, inexpensive formula that promotes a beautiful coat and helps repel fleas on both dogs and cats. Simply pour 2 cups of boiling water over 1 teaspoon of dried rosemary and steep for ten minutes, covered. Strain and cool to body temperature. Rub this into your pet's coat and gently towel dry without further rinsing. Your pet will look, feel, and smell great, and wow, what a shine! I'm also a fan of tea tree oil and aloe vera, which have soothing topical effects when applied to the skin or any irritated areas.

Eyes, Ears, and Noses

Animals rely on their keen senses of sight, sound, and smell, so you need to be especially gentle and treat the sensory organs on your pet's face with great care. Never use anything that seems to aggravate an existing problem.

Some breeds of animals are predisposed to certain chronic eye, ear, or nose issues and might require more specialized care of these body parts. For example, pets bred to have "peke" or pushed-in faces, such as Pekingese, pugs, or Persian cats, may be born with bent tear ducts. Debris can get clogged in the bend and then waste backs up in the tear duct, sometimes spilling out on the face and producing a chronic discharge. These kinds of animals need more regular eye care, but the good news is that the tear stains and discharge can easily be kept under control with a simple saline solution that helps unclog the ducts, leaving them clean and refreshed.

Some eye stains or discharge could be caused by allergies to chemicals in your house or around the yard. An herbal rinse will never hurt, but a chronic condition that doesn't go away, even after changing the diet, should be checked out by your holistic vet to make sure nothing is stuck in your pet's eye or behind the lid.

A word of caution: Never use any commercial saline solutions for contact lenses in a pet's eye. Chemical preservatives must be used in commercial saline solutions to ensure that bacteria don't grow in the bottle. These chemicals can be so caustic and damaging to the eye that manufacturers use chemical anesthetics in their products to eliminate any pain caused by the preservative. It's always better to make up your own fresh, natural saline solutions as needed.

Anitra Frazier recommends a two-step eyewash using eyebright and goldenseal to remedy any eye problems and cleanse the eyes. It's soothing and gentle and makes *all* eyes feel good. I love using the eyebright solution in my own eyes, especially if I've been on the computer too long. You can purchase her remedy premade or make it yourself.

ANITRA'S HERBAL EYEWASH

Yield: 1 cup / Serving Size: See usage directions

BORIC ACID/EYEBRIGHT SOLUTION

1 cup distilled water or springwater

$^1/_2$ teaspoon boric acid

1 drop eyebright extract

Heat the water and add the boric acid. Stir until dissolved and let cool. To soothe red tissue: Add 1 drop of eyebright extract to 1 tablespoon of the boric acid solution. Put 2 drops of the boric acid/eyebright solution into each eye once or twice daily. After using this solution for 3 days, make the saline solution below.

SALINE/GOLDENSEAL SOLUTION

1 cup distilled water or springwater

$^1/_2$ teaspoon salt

1 drop goldenseal extract

Heat the water and add the salt. Stir until dissolved and let cool. To shrink swollen tissue and disinfect: Add 1 drop of goldenseal extract to 1 tablespoon of the saline solution. Put 2 drops of the saline/goldenseal solution into each eye once or twice daily. After using this solution for 3 days, use the boric acid/eyebright solution for another 3 days.

Note: Your eyewashes will only keep for three days. Discard any leftover solution and make a new batch as needed. Make sure anything you put into your pet's body is either room temperature or just slightly above, never hot or cold.

Pets with long, floppy, or hairy ears are more prone to ear infections and wax buildup. But regardless of whether ears stick up, flop down, or fold, they need to be lovingly cleaned and cared for. Your pet will let you know when its ears have a problem. If your pet shakes its head, digs in its ear with a back foot, or rubs its ears on carpets and sofas, these are sure signs that something needs your attention. Black specks in the ears may indicate ear mites, and an unpleasant odor is definitely a sign that there's an issue. A conscientious owner observes and analyzes. The sooner you detect a problem, the easier and quicker it will be to remedy, and the less your pet will suffer. Try making up a batch of Voyko's herbal ear wash to soothe and eliminate most any ear problem. The ingredients in this effective ear relief remedy are available in most health food stores.

VOYKO'S EAR WASH

Yield: About 3 ounces / Serving Size: See usage directions

2 ounces witch hazel

5 drops tea tree oil

5 drops clove oil

Mix all of the ingredients together in a clean bottle. If the liquid is cold, it may be uncomfortable for your pet, so before using it, warm the bottle in your hands for a minute or two until it's a nice soothing body temperature, or place the bottle in a cup of warm water to take off the chill. Squirt half an eyedropper into one ear. Try to do it quickly, then gently fold the earflap over and massage for thirty seconds. Afterward, let your pet shake it out, then treat the other ear.

TOSS OUT

Yet again, get rid of anything not 100 percent herbal and natural. Watch out for chemicals, alcohols, and anything that doesn't feel soothing or gentle on you. Before I use anything new on any of my pets, I try it out on myself first. That way, I'm always sure how it will affect them. If it feels good to me, it's probably going to feel good to them, too.

I've always made it a practice to thoroughly test all of my products on humans before trying them on pets. People have the wonderful ability to articulate and describe how something feels, and if something doesn't feel good, we can communicate that and do something about it right away. Since animals can't tell us how they feel, and since they generally can't wash off something that doesn't feel good, they're much more likely to suffer if products aren't gentle and soothing. And remember, if it doesn't feel good, your pet will probably try to get rid of the sensation by licking and grooming itself, so they may end up ingesting whatever is in the product. I never took chances with my own product line and insisted that everything used feel gentle and soothing on all of my own body parts.

LOOK FOR

Choose eye and ear products emphasizing witch hazel, chamomile, clove, goldenseal, and eyebright. Your eyes, ears, and nose are all connected, and combinations of those ingredients (in their diluted forms) will prove most effective for gently soothing irritations and providing antibacterial and antifungal effects.

Chronic eye and ear problems are symptoms of the body's gallant efforts to eliminate toxins, which can be expelled through all of the body's orifices. These problems are often an indication that the body is working hard to eliminate wastes due to poor-quality foods and chemicals. The eyes, ears, and nose provide easy channels for the body to remove waste, but once you stop feeding your pet antagonistic elements, like overly processed foods and chemicals, these conditions often clear up within days. The story of Blondie illustrates this well.

Blondie and Diane: All Ears

Diane found Blondie, an adorable, four-month-old blonde cocker spaniel, playing by herself at the pet store. Because she was a bit older than the other puppies in the pen, the store owner was offering her at half price to sell her more quickly. All her life, Diane had wanted a dog, and now the timing was perfect: her children were grown and she was living alone. It had never occurred to Diane that this particular pet, being of dubious breeding, came predisposed to all kinds of health problems. (Diane found out much later that the store had purchased this dog from a puppy mill. I caution people seeking purebred pets to find out where and how they were bred. Too many hearts have been broken because of sick puppies and kittens who were inbred at incompetent or inhumane breeding facilities.)

Blondie had chronic weepy eyes and her otherwise beautiful face seemed to always be stained even though Diane gingerly wiped the discharge from the corners of Blondie's eyes every morning. With their long, floppy ears, cocker spaniels are also predisposed to all kinds of ear problems. When air can't get in, bacteria tend to grow, so they often require more focused ear hygiene as part of their regular grooming. Although Diane was as gentle and loving as possible, Blondie always tried to bite her during ear-care sessions, and this was understandably very upsetting.

Even the trainer had no remedy for the unruly behavior Blondie often displayed, and Diane became frightened at the thought of Blondie biting her grandkids if they played a little too rough. It never occurred to Diane that pain was the reason for Blondie's aggressiveness; she always assumed it was more psychological than physical. She tried twenty-seven different ear medications over the course of eight months, and all had at least four things in common. All the products were expensive. None worked to eliminate the awful odor that constantly plagued the poor dog. The products were all greasy (most commercial products for ears are actually oil based, which makes no sense and actually defeats the purpose when try-ing to clean the ears). And lastly, all the products caused pain—a huge drawback as grooming is no fun for anyone when the pet must be chased, held down, and muzzled to get the job done.

I urged Diane to start cooking natural foods for Blondie and told her about the magical healing properties of EFAs in the diet. Keeping Blondie's food wholesome and letting the fatty acids do their job of cleaning out the digestive tract would help to remove the debris that was clogging her system and enable her body to flush the toxins out through normal channels.

Once Blondie's diet changed, it took only a few days for the eye dis-charge to stop. But the real challenge was in dealing with her ears. I recommended a soothing herbal ear wash made with several extracts, including chamomile and clove, in a witch hazel base, and to Diane and Blondie's immense relief, it immediately stopped all the pain. For the first time in Blondie's life, she expressed a huge sigh of relief when her ears were massaged with this gentle preparation. Diane was astounded that she could even get close enough to touch those places that previously aggravated Blondie so, and was deeply grateful to accomplish the task with all her fingers intact!

Blondie now looks forward to her weekly grooming session with Diane. It's an extraordinary opportunity for the two of them to spend quality time together, and Blondie just loves her three-minute ear massage, which keeps her ears clean and fresh. She's even been known to make soft humming noises as her ears are lovingly rubbed. As a bonus, Diane discovered that the herbal ear wash was actually a refreshing addition to her own after-shower regime, as well.

Healing Salves and Ointments

You have likely used topical ointments, salves, lotions, creams, and even antibiotics as treatments for your pet. As always, and at the risk of being redundant, diet is a major player related to skin irritations, excessive itching, gnawing, and hot spots. Many holistic vets start their treatments for these problems with a brief fast of chicken broth before introducing a more hearty natural diet and addressing symptoms. Cold-pressed oils rich in essential fatty acids can prove equally effective in addressing the problem internally. When you work on an area topically, look for products that include vitamins A, D, and E to help soothe irritated areas, and read labels carefully. Products applied to the skin should soothe, cleanse, and heal, and a good way to test whether they do so is to try them on your own skin.

When applying anything to your pet's skin (particularly with cats), try not to get anything greasy on its fur. Work on a small area at a time and part the hair well so you get down to the skin, where the treatment is needed most. Since cats are so fastidious, it's best not to leave them feeling soiled.

Vegetable oils such as soy, almond, or coconut can be very healing when used topically. Beeswax, aloe vera, vitamin E, tea tree oil, and lavender oil are all beneficial to the skin and have antifungal and antibacterial properties. I'm crazy about the antiseptic and healing abilities of calendula, comfrey, and myrrh. You can try any of these natural substances topically on the skin, separately, or combined for best results.

Flea and Tick Control Products

The best advice in regard to fleas and ticks can be encapsulated in two words: *flea comb*. This is the most underrated, underappreciated, and undervalued grooming aid. A great flea comb, which will last a lifetime, is your best defense against parasites. Use it daily to spot-check your furry friend for any other parasites, too, such as ticks or worms. When grooming your pet and searching for fleas, keep a dish of soapy water next to you. When you catch a flea, simply dunk it in the water. Fleas actually smother in the soapy solution, and with each flea you catch, you're one step closer to a healthier dog or cat. Fleas won't stand a chance against your own personal weapon of mass destruction.

Though most cats don't like to be combed backward, with dogs you can also gently run the comb backward to find any critters hiding in the deeper fur or darker areas. Regular combing and brushing will also help to stimulate the skin's oil glands and bring a healthy, natural shine to the skin and coat. That in combination with topical insect-repelling herbs and extracts can keep fleas and ticks at bay no matter where you live or what time of year. Even better, with a truly healthy diet, your well-fed pet won't attract fleas unless its immune system becomes compromised.

It's also a great idea to invest in a good vacuum cleaner. If you have a temporary flea infestation, you'll want to keep your house cleaned and vacuumed every day. Consider this fact, which is scary but true: about 10 percent of the fleas are the ones you see on your pet; the other 90 percent are in the environment in the forms of eggs and larvae. So use the deep setting for your carpets and also vacuum anywhere eggs or larvae might be: underneath the sofa cushions, anywhere your pet sleeps or grooms itself, and even out on the porch or patio.

If you're not sure if your cat or dog has fleas, brush your pet gently and examine a few loose hairs. If you see little black specks that look like pepper, your pet may just be dirty, but it could be fleas. To find out, lay the hairs on a wet white paper towel, then fold it and press firmly. After a minute, unfold the paper towel and examine the debris. If the specks have left what look like rust marks on the paper towel, your pet does have fleas. What you're seeing is the flea excrement, along with your pet's dried blood. It's time to take action!

TOSS OUT

Avoid any product with fenthion, cythioate, or imidacloprid because of the neurotoxic effects they can have on cats or puppies. I list these because they are prominent in popular monthly topical flea treatments. However, the real mystery to me is that the government allows the manufacturers to use all manner of inert ingredients without listing them. Isn't it a wonder that you can read a product label that clearly lists "active ingredients" as separate items but lumps the hidden, mysterious ones under "and other inert ingredients." That amorphous category makes up 75 to 90 percent of the pesticides in flea and tick products. Don't be fooled by the term *inert.* According to the Environmental Protection Agency (EPA), U.S. law only requires "active" ingredients to be reported, even though they freely admit that many of these "inert" ingredients have *known* adverse human, animal, and environmental effects. Of course, the EPA recommends that you follow instructions, and many products advise you to wear gloves, open windows, not get the product in your eyes or on clothing, keep out of reach of children, wash your hands thoroughly after use, and so on. Sadly, they then instruct you to thoroughly soak or dust your pet with their product and leave it on indefinitely.

Here's my rule of thumb: if a product has chemicals or pesticides that are harmful to you, it's harmful to your pet. Toss it out! I've seen the damage these chemicals have done on too many pets. Not only can they burn the skin where applied, they seep into the bloodstream, make their way to internal organs, and compromise the immune system and overall well-being. If you still feel you must use chemical-laden products, take the time to learn the signs of overdose and long-term effects of the chemical ingredients. Call the manufacturers and ask for the Material Safety Data Sheet (MSDS) on each of their ingredients. Read the inserts that come with products, and heed all the warning statements. But hopefully all of that trouble and the frightening facts you learn will convince you to just go natural; it's simpler and safer.

LOOK FOR

Many natural botanicals have been used for centuries for controlling pests. Try essential oils of cedarwood, citronella, eucalyptus, juniper, lavender, lemongrass, orange, peppermint, pine needle, rosemary, sage, or tea tree oil. You can mix $1/8$ teaspoon of any of these essential oils with 16 ounces of liquid castile soap for use as a natural flea shampoo. For a great herbal collar, place a few drops of any of these oils on the top (outer) side of a cloth, a bandana, or other porous collar to help repel fleas. (Don't allow the undiluted form of any of these essential oils to directly contact your pet's skin, as some of them could cause irritation.) Your pet will smell luscious, and the herbs will help keep pests away. For a spectacular after-bath rinse, mix $1/8$ teaspoon of peppermint oil with 3 cups of water in a spray bottle and mist your pets, its sleeping areas, and any other problem areas around the house. Your pet will smell like a delicious little peppermint pattie, and the solution helps keep fleas away.

HEALTHY PETS DON'T HAVE FLEAS!

Grooming isn't about fleas; it's about beauty, health, and cleanliness. Ridding your pets of fleas or ticks is a wonderful by-product of all the changes you've made over the last eight weeks. As you've learned, a healthy coat and skin require real, nutrient-dense food, especially great sources of protein, essential fatty acids, and vitamins. A poor-quality diet leads to an unhealthy skin and coat and a compromised immune system, which in turn attracts fleas and ticks like bees to honey. Applying toxic chemicals to the skin of a pet with an already compromised immune system only perpetuates the downward health cycle. The weaker the animal, the stronger the fleas become.

During times of stress or weakness, the immune system can become compromised, and any animal may wind up a fat meal for fleas or ticks. This is one of nature's ways of cleaning up the weak and inferior; parasites are attracted to anything in a weakened state of health. Picture a garden: hearty plants never attract parasites, but weaker ones do. The same holds true for pets and people. Parasites always prefer weak, old, and sick animals. Therefore, if your pet has a flea problem, you know its immune system needs a boost in the nutrient department. Make sure you're not leaving food down during the day; this slows the metabolism and backs up wastes, and excessive waste in your pet's system attracts more fleas. Make sure you supplement with essential fatty acids and vitamin C for optimum skin health, too. Fleas are more attracted to unhealthy, dry skin and dandruff. They like to bury themselves deep in those scaly areas.

As always, remember to address your pet's environment, too. Don't forget to launder its bedding often. Vacuum your house regularly, and dispose of the vacuum bags after each use if you have a flea problem. Take them out of your home. If you don't, flea eggs will hatch in the vacuum bags, allowing these pests to invade your home again.

Krissy, Sugar, and Baby: The Flea-Free Three

Krissy, an enthusiastic twenty-four-year-old legal assistant, couldn't wait to move to Florida and set up her new house and run with her dogs on the beach. It was a particularly stressful time for her, but she maintained it was an excellent career change, and she was buzzing with excitement for weeks. The boxes were packed, all the arrangements were made, and she and her two devoted brown and tan shepherd mixes, Sugar and Baby, boarded the plane that would take them from Delaware to their adorable cottage on the bay. Krissy had always been meticulous about her dogs' care. Well-read and into nutrition herself, Krissy understood the importance of making their food, and she gave them vitamins and lots of exercise to provide them the healthiest life possible. Up to now it had worked, but Krissy worried how they would fare in the hot Florida climate, where she'd heard fleas could be a year-round problem.

Sometimes, no matter how many ducks you have in a row, you can't get around Murphy's Law, and Krissy couldn't have anticipated all the setbacks she would encounter with her move. Everything that could go wrong did. The movers, painters, and utility companies all prevented her from starting her new job on time. The stress was rapidly building, and although she understood that all the setbacks were temporary, she couldn't shake the worry that engulfed her new life.

Equally unnerving, both dogs were like sponges and absorbed all the anxiety that their mom exuded. The stress took its toll, and within days the dogs developed the worst case of fleas imaginable. By the end of the first week, they were itching and scratching and had become horribly infested. Krissy's convictions presented yet another stressor, as she felt pressured to deal with the flea problem as holistically as possible. With everything else that was going on, it seemed it would be easier to just bomb the house and dip her dogs. Although it was more work, Krissy decided to stick to her holistic approach. She felt that the first line of defense was to boost her dogs' immune systems by doubling up on their vitamins. Her weapons of choice were a double dose of vitamin C and more EFAs, raw foods, and greens. The health food store suggested an aromatic castile shampoo with eucalyptus and citronella to help smother and repel the fleas. She took great care to keep the entire house clean, but the most useful tools were the flea comb and the vacuum cleaner. Krissy took out all her aggressions and anger on the pests that plagued her dogs' world as she proceeded to drown them one at a time in soapy water.

Thankfully, it took only fourteen days to turn the situation around. The dogs got cleaned up, regained all their energy, and never suffered with another bout of fleas again. Krissy started her job, and the house turned out fine. She was finally able to focus on all the reasons they had moved—for all that positive energy created by their daily swim in the ocean and romps on the sandy, white beaches. Life can be perfect in paradise, as long as everyone's healthy!

Doggie Day Spa and Kitty Couture

This spa day is all about indulgence and pampering. You'll take some quality time to move, stretch, and play, then follow up with a thorough brushing and body massage. You'll trim your pet's nails, check its eyes, ears, and nose, and get your furry friend thoroughly clean with a soothing herb-infused bath and a rosemary rinse.

THE DAY BEFORE

Gather all the items in the list below. If necessary, make a shopping trip to get anything you don't have on hand. Here's what you'll need:

- Dried rosemary

- Peppermint essential oil

- A spray bottle for your peppermint spritz

- Castile shampoo

- Your pet's favorite brush

- Wide-toothed grooming comb

- Flea comb (if needed)

- Anitra's Herbal Eyewash, if needed (page 213)

- Voyko's Ear Wash (page 214)

- Cotton balls

- Gauze pads

- Calendula oil, almond oil, or vitamin E oil

- Safe pet nail clippers

- An old towel to put in the sink (for cats)

- Several plush, soft cotton towels for drying

- A blow-dryer

- Treats and bottled springwater for the break

THE SPA DAY

Prepare your rosemary rinse and peppermint finishing spritz in advance (see pages 211 and 220). Next, spend some quality time with your pet. If you have a dog, go outside for a leisurely walk together. If you have a cat, spend fifteen minutes quietly petting your cat and talking to it. This will help energize you for the tasks ahead, create a trusting and comfortable closeness, and fine-tune the atmosphere for your animal friend. Enjoy the tranquility of the morning, breathe deeply, and center yourself and your pet during this special time together. You may want to light scented candles and let the room fill with lovely aromas that make you feel good. (For safety's sake, place the candles high up out of harm's way.)

Now it's time for a light massage. As you feel your way through your pet's coat, remove any stickers or burrs and check for fleas and skin irritations all over the body, including the genital areas. Start with your pet's face, then caress its ears, rub its neck, and gently work your way through its entire body. Give special attention to all of the joints, including the hips. This is one of the simplest, most pleasurable acts you can do for yourself and your pet. Take your time and enjoy the massage. See if you can gracefully encourage your pet to lie down on its side, then gently stretch all four legs forward and back. It's a great idea to massage each leg from the thighs to the ankles and each toe individually.

As you work your way over your pet's entire body, you'll get to know your pet more intimately, noticing its every inch. Breathe deeply and enjoy the pleasure your pet is experiencing. The good energy you're creating for your pet can be transferred back to you if you let it come through. Enjoy the process; this is your spa day, too. Giving a gentle full massage is a wonderful way to get your cat more accustomed to the lovely ritual of touch. Most cats seem to enjoy it, but each cat is as individual as its owner—so let your kitty be your guide. Observe closely what it likes best and what pleases it most. You can strengthen your bond with every touch.

Now give your pet's coat a thorough, detailed brushing. For dogs, pick up your pet's favorite brush or comb and start counting—100 strokes from top to bottom. (Don't forget to gently back-brush a longer-haired dog.) Brushing helps remove dead hair and skin and spreads natural oils throughout the coat. If you find a mat or a knot, use a comb and work it out gently. You may need to enlist the help of a professional groomer for this task. If you're inexperienced or nervous, don't try to cut out any knots yourself or bathe an animal that has become seriously matted. You could hurt your pet, and the experience may make both of you fearful of any future sessions together. Don't be afraid to get help from a local holistic groomer and carefully observe them as they handle your pet. Ask questions so that you'll be better equipped to do it yourself the next time. Your confidence in working with your pet will speak volumes to it emotionally.

For cats, I like to sit cross-legged on the bed with my cat in my lap facing away from me. As I brush it ever so lovingly, I speak to it softly to help build its confidence. Sometimes I enlist the help of a wide-toothed comb, which my cats have learned to love, too. If you encounter fleas, now is the best time to bring out the flea comb and the dish of soapy water I talked about a little earlier in the chapter. Always use short, careful strokes, and make sure that you never pull or tug the hair. Remember that cats are sensitive and pulling on mats or tangles can hurt. Carefully and methodically, make sure that you cover your cat's entire body, and try to stroke and pet it as much as possible throughout the process. Once your cat gets used to this lovely ritual, it may even ask you to do it some more!

After you've finished brushing and combing, check your pet's eyes, ears, and nose. Its eyes should be clear, clean, and bright. Check the whites, too. Bloodshot whites are a definite sign of irritation. If the eyes are crusty or have secretions, now's the time to use Anitra's Herbal Eyewash, as described on page 213.

Your pet's ears should be clean, fresh, and free of wax. No matter what condition your pet's ears are in, give them a healing treatment with Voyko's Ear Wash, as described on page 214. You can also saturate a cotton ball with the ear wash and gently wipe around the outer part of the ear. But please, never probe into a pet's ear canal with a cotton swab. It's all too easy to injure their sensitive ear canal if you push even a little too far.

For cats, after you've cleaned out the ears you can gently position a cotton ball in each ear opening. Place it in just far enough to not fall out. This will help at bath time, in just a few minutes. The cotton will help reduce water noise a bit and also keep water from getting in the ears. It won't hurt if your pet gets water in its ears, but it does makes the bathing experiencing less comfortable, especially for a cat.

Your pet's nose should be free of debris and dirt. Wipe away any secretions with a soft cloth or piece of gauze dipped in warm water, then pat the nose dry with a soft towel. To soften hardened secretions, you can dab on a bit of almond oil, vitamin E oil, or calendula oil. It may take two or three sessions to remove anything hardened around the nose, so be patient; you don't want to irritate this sensitive area.

If you are thoroughly comfortable with clipping your pet's nails and have the proper tools, include this in your spa treatment. If you've never done this before but would like to learn how, have a professional groomer show you. Using the wrong technique could hurt your pet or make it afraid of any grooming tool. You might want to work up to this delicate operation by giving your dog or cat a foot massage on a regular basis to get it accustomed to having its feet touched and make clipping its nails much easier.

Keeping nails trimmed can be critical for a dog's well-being. When a dog's nails are neglected for too long, they may overgrow and the dog could end up with crippling and painful malformations of their toes and feet. You can help prevent this with proper diet and appropriate grooming. Before trimming a dog's nails, massage the paws and make note of any irregularities or sore spots. Then squeeze each toe gently to release the nail to its outermost position before clipping.

To keep your cat's claws naturally healthy, trimmed, and in peak condition, make sure you provide them with a sturdy scratching post. The clawing action enables them to condition their nails themselves without you ever having to cut them. The post also acts as a great deterrent to keep them from scratching up your furniture. I have three great scratching posts in my home, strategically placed near all my fine furniture. Many cats need help with their nails, and a human toenail clipper works very well. Be very careful to avoid clipping too close to the cuticle. A little snip off the tip of the claw is enough. Don't be surprised if you can't get to each claw in only one session, and be conscious of your cat's tolerance levels.

You've both sat still long enough; it's time for a shift in position. A refreshing drink of fresh springwater is definitely in order for both of you. Also consider a short play session, a fabulous treat, or even a little cat (or dog) nap. Read your pet's body language and ask it what it would like to do next. Remember that this is supposed to be a relaxing and luxurious day for everyone. Take your time and don't rush the process. It's about spending a day with your beloved pet and focusing on health, well-being, and comfort.

Now it's time to let the bathing begin. It's all about pampering and pleasure. The best tool for bathing is a gentle spray nozzle on the end of a flexible hose. The water should be warm; run it over your wrist to ensure it's a comfortable, moderate temperature. If a variety of settings are an option, choose the one that puts water out in a soft, steady stream. Keep the spray head as close to your pet's body as possible so the water doesn't squirt out and splatter into its eyes, nose, or ears, which can be terribly uncomfortable. Always keep a few extra cotton towels nearby. Whisper, coo, and compliment your pet on how beautiful it is, and how much better it's going to feel because of this loving bath.

For dogs, the tub or a shower will do nicely. I like to get into the shower with my dogs because it makes it easier for me to maneuver. I can kneel down easily to get all of those hard-to-reach places, and there's less strain on my back.

Always bathe a cat in a tall sink, keeping it as close to you as possible, and line the bottom of the sink with an old towel. This will prevent the cat from slipping or sliding and give them something soft for their paws and claws to hold onto. It helps make them more confident and provides more stability. Never place a cat in water deeper than its ankles. Even a shallow pool of water can be frightening to them.

Gently wet your pet's body down with warm water. Then, starting at the top of its head, apply herbal shampoo to its neck and head, chest, shoulders, front legs, back, tummy, hind legs, paws, and tail. Be very careful to avoid its eyes, nose, and mouth, and be gentle but thorough around the genitals. Keep your pet's comfort foremost in your mind. Massage gently all over its body using lots of circular motions. Keep warm water handy and flowing at all times and apply more warm water if your pet becomes chilled.

When you're finished shampooing, rinse away all the suds by keeping the spray nozzle right against the body. Continuously moving a gentle stream of warm water over the whole body, carefully rinse every body part, using one hand to massage and help guide the soapy solution off and away from the body. Make sure that you rinse every inch of your pet and that all shampoo is washed away, but be extremely careful around the eyes, ears, and nose. Keep talking to your pet quietly and happily and let it know how beautifully it's doing and how much its good behavior pleases you. Give nose-to-nose Eskimo kisses often and tell your pet how great it smells now. Make sure your pet hears how happy it makes you to see it so clean and healthy. Be sure to rinse well!

Now it's time for conditioner. Put the rosemary rinse into a plastic bowl, and gently pour it over your pet's back, down its neck, and around its rump. Work the aromatic solution through the entire coat with your fingers and breathe deeply, as this lovely infusion will have calming and therapeutic properties for both of you.

Dry your pet gently by wrapping it in a soft, warm towel. This is also a good time to remove the cotton from your cat's ears. After the towel has sopped up a fair amount of water, allow your dog to shake vigorously. Some cats like to do this too. Using another towel, wrap your pet again and repeat the process until most of the water is off of its coat. The more towels you use, the faster the drying process. Then, to top off the comfort, use a handheld blow-dryer on a very low heat. Always direct the dryer so it blows partly on your own hand so you can constantly ensure a comfortably warm heat level. Never touch the dryer nozzle to your pet's skin or coat; it could burn or cause irritation. Start the process at the hind legs and move up the body slowly.

Keep the dryer moving constantly, and with your free hand either fluff the coat with your fingers or use a brush your pet finds comfortable. Brush gently and continue to pat softly until your pet's coat is almost entirely dry, especially in the winter, so it doesn't get a chill.

When drying a cat, you may want to have an assistant to expedite the process. The fastest way to complete your session is to have a friend hold your cat in a towel on his or her lap while you use the blow-dryer and towel together. Never try to comb a long-haired cat when it's still wet. The hair mats too easily, so it would be very painful and the outcome would be awful for all of you.

Finish off your delightful ritual with a light peppermint spritz. For dogs, use the mist setting and generously spray your dog from tip to toe. For cats, it's best not to spray the peppermint spritz. The bottle produces a hissing sound, which will probably frighten your cat. Instead, pour the solution on your own hands, then lightly caress and pet your cat's entire coat.

Now relax, kick back, and enjoy the amazing aromas permeating your home. Pick a warm, sunny spot if you can, and enjoy some clean, quiet time together.

Dog Tip: A dog may become so excited after the long, luxury spa treatment that it may need to relieve itself. Invite your dog to go out for a walk if it wants, before you settle down for some sleepy time together.

By now, you and your pet should be feeling totally transformed. Breathe deeply, look around, and appreciate the results of your spa day. Then look deeper and notice how much you've accomplished in just eight short weeks. If you've followed all of the steps in the program, it's likely that your pet's life and health have changed dramatically.

Week Eight Assessment

❑ What grooming products did you toss this week? What ingredients did those products contain that prompted your concern? Are you still using commercial body care products for yourself, or did this week's project mean big changes for you, too?

❑ Is your pet genetically prone to certain problems, such as in its eyes or ears? If so, are you ready to incorporate gentle remedies into your pet's regimen to help it feel, look, and smell better?

❑ Did you take your time and enjoy the spa day? What part of it did your pet seem to love most? How much time did you take on your spa day to luxuriate in the pleasurable comfort of the aromatic therapies? Did it seem like enough time?

❑ As you ran your hands over your pet's entire body, did you find any sore spots or sensitive areas? Describe any lingering problems and what you plan to do about them.

Daily Play

This is the last time I get to ask; from now on, you'll have to be diligent on your own. Did you make your daily playtimes? You found time to play with your pet at least twice a day for at least ten minutes each session, right? My pets give me hints when they want me to play, bringing me their favorite pull toy, catnip ball, stick, bone, whatever. Now that you're at the end of this eight-week program, you should be very tuned in and sensitive to your pet and pick up on similar cues.

Cat Play Tip: You can definitely stimulate your cat, both mentally and physically, with an inexpensive little gizmo—a laser pointer pen. They just love scooting across the floor and up and over the furniture in hot pursuit of that point of light. I've seen even the most sedentary cats get hopped up over this toy, and it's fun for the whole family. *Caution:* Please make sure you never shine the light directly into any pet's or person's eyes.

Dog Play Tip: Here's my all-time favorite dog play tip: look at your dog and smile warmly. Clap your hands and tell your pup what a great friend it is. When I do this, my dogs know I'm excited and that it's playtime. We all benefit holistically from play, so . . . just do it.

◆ ◆ ◆

You've completed the eight-week program. Now it's time to take your third Pet Portrait and see how much your pet has improved. Once you've done so, go back and compare it with the first portrait, and then week five's portrait. Reread your journal and make notes summarizing everything you've learned.

I urge you to continue keenly observing your pet by keeping up your journal and taking periodic Whole Pet Portraits throughout your pet's life. Document all of your pet's important milestones with words, photos, and videos. Remember to step back and admire your masterpiece often, for it is ever changing. What you feed your pet, how much you feed, and what its body needs to help it age gracefully will always be evolving. Your pet is always changing, and with love and wisdom you can respond to these changes and help your companion be as healthy and happy as it can be. I know you wouldn't have it any other way. After all, your best friend helps you be the best that you can be, too.

Conclusion:
Everything Is Pawsible!

Canine congratulations and feline felicitations: you've transitioned your pet through the Whole Pet Diet program. By now you've likely witnessed the incredible metamorphosis of an animal you love. As you notice the outside of its body changing—the texture of its coat or the condition of its skin—understand that your companion's inside is becoming healthier as well. Newly found energy, weight loss, and a more joyful disposition should show you that your pet is becoming increasingly stronger and healthier every day. All of this should provide wonderful motivation to perpetuate the new, healthier lifestyle.

I applaud you wholeheartedly for approaching your pet's health and well-being from a standpoint that may have seemed foreign at the outset. Change can be frightening, and embracing the unknown takes great strength. But by now, you understand that improving your pet's health doesn't take a degree in biology, and it's no mystery to you that real, fresh food, a chemical-free lifestyle, and vitamins can bolster the body's natural ability to heal.

Feel free to share your journey on my website (www.thewholepet-diet.com). Post your own recipes, relate true pet stories, and ask questions so that others may benefit from your insights. The website is also full of resources you might find helpful: useful books, links to my favorite websites, new product reviews, and detailed information about products I make, use, or recommend.

Continue to take Whole Pet Portraits throughout your pet's life. You are more in control of its health and well-being than ever before. If you stray from the principles outlined in this book, you can always refer to your journal and get back on track. Remember that for any being, it's never too late to eat well.

Recommended
Resources

Knowledge is power, and I encourage you to learn as much as you can about holistic pet care to help you make better choices. As you begin to digest this program and develop an appetite for more, I recommend the following books and resources. Consult them often.

Allegretti, Jan, and Katy Sommers. *The Complete Holistic Dog Book: Home Health Care for Our Canine Companions.* Berkeley, CA: Celestial Arts, 2003.

American Holistic Veterinary Medical Association. www.ahvma.org. Provides journals for members, and seminars and conferences in holistic animal care.

Balch, Phyllis, and James Balch. *Prescription for Nutritional Healing.* 3rd ed. New York: Penguin Putnam, 2000.

Belfield, Wendell O., and Martin Zucker. *How to Have a Healthier Dog.* New York: Signet/Doubleday, 1981.

Belfield, Wendell O., and Martin Zucker. *The Very Healthy Cat Book.* San Jose, CA: Orthomolecular Specialties, 1983.

Bremness, Lesley. *The Complete Book of Herbs: A Practical Guide to Growing and Using Herbs.* New York: Viking Studio Books, 1988.

Clark, Hulda Regehr. *The Cure for All Cancers.* San Diego, CA: ProMotion Publishing, 1993.

Crowley, Nancy. "The Whole Pet: Natural Flea and Tick Repellants." *Spirit of Change Magazine.* October 18, 2005.

Frazier, Anitra, and Norma Eckroate. *The New Natural Cat: A Complete Guide for Finicky Owners.* New York: Plume, 1990.

Goldstein, Martin. *The Nature of Animal Healing: The Path to Your Pet's Health, Happiness, and Longevity.* New York: Random House, 1999.

Herb Research Foundation. www.herbs.org. Dedicated to the use of herbs as food and medicine.

Loeb, Paul, and Jo Loeb. *Cathletics: Ways to Amuse and Exercise Your Cat.* Secaucus, NJ: Castle, 1981.

Martin, Ann M. *Food Pets Die For: Shocking Facts about Pet Food.* Troutdale, OR: New Sage Press, 1997.

Messonnier, Shawn. *Natural Health Bible for Dogs and Cats.* New York: Prima Publishing, 2001.

Neighborhood Cats. www.neighborhoodcats.org. A great resource for learning more about trap-neuter-return methods of managing feral cat populations.

Pitcairn, Richard H., and S. H. Pitcairn. *Dr. Pitcairn's Complete Guide to Natural Health for Dogs and Cats.* Emmaus, PA: Rodale, 2005.

Pitchford, Paul. *Healing with Whole Foods: Asian Traditions and Modern Nutrition.* Berkeley, CA: North Atlantic Books, 2002.

Schwartz, Cheryl. *Natural Healing for Dogs and Cats A-Z.* Carlsbad, CA: Hay House, 2000.

Vanderhaeghe, Lorna R., and Patrick J. D. Bouic. *The Immune System Cure.* New York: Kensington Books, 1999.

Veterinary Institute of Integrative Medicine. www.viim.org. Articles and research on the blending of allopathic and naturopathic medicine.

About the Author

Andi Brown's mission for the past twenty years has been to educate the public about holistic pet care using real, wholesome, fresh, and natural foods. An avid pet lover and pet health care advocate, Andi is an acclaimed writer and the director of Halo, Purely for Pets, the only company in the world making pet care products that are safe and approved for humans, too! She's touched the hearts and bellies of hundreds of thousands of now-healthy pets and their loyal companions. You can read her column "The Holistic Dog" and "The Holistic Cat" in various pet fancier and human health publications. Andi lives in Florida with two beautiful dogs, two fabulous cats, and the master chef who helped create it all.

Index